Escape from Utah

by Carla Eggman-Garrett

RED LEAD PRESS
PITTSBURGH, PENNSYLVANIA 15222

For more information or to order additional books, please contact:
Red Lead Press
701 Smithfield Street
Pittsburgh, Pennsylvania 15222
U.S.A.
1-800-834-1803
www.redleadbooks.com

Contents

Chapter 1

The Final Goodbye

My head was in my ex-husbands' lap. We had been divorced for two years and were talking of reconciling. We still had a strong attraction to each other and wanted to see if we could still get together again. We were in the seat of his yellow '72 El Camino he had purchased the year our daughter, Ann, was born. "Are you coming back after you go to Brigham Young University?" he asked pensively. "You know that is where every one goes to get married to other Mormons."

The night had a fully beautiful June moon, and we were parked in front of his mother's mansion. The moon was glowing on the house and the beautiful garden. "No," I replied. "I have no intention of getting married at BY Woo," (the affectionate Mormon name used in place of BYU for Mormons sending their 'choice' daughters and sons to get married to other 'choice' members of their church.) I will be back at the end of the summer, and we will talk about getting married again."

"I'll write to you," he said softly.

"I'll write back," I returned.

"Take care of Annie," he stated in a concerned voice.

"I will," I answered.

Even then, inside my head, a voice was screaming, "What about his mother?"

At this, Vince seemed relieved, and drove me back to my Mercury Cougar I left at a filling station in Sultana.

I still felt unnerved about being around the mansion after living there with his mother. This is where I had the 'divorce party' when Vince and his mother got their divorce from me. Vince and I could never see eye on religion. I wanted a temple marriage, a marriage that had been pounded into my head ever since I was a young girl. My mother and father had a temple marriage, even though they were not the always the most blissful couple in the world. Indeed, because of the fights my mom and dad had, I don't think I knew what a "good" marriage was. My father was abusive to my mother and all of our family. But I had to be married in the Mormon temple to be 'sealed' to that person forever.

I had discussed a 'Temple' marriage to Vince on many occasions hoping he would change his mind. Of course, he was hoping I would change my mind and join the Catholic Church and get married to him in that church. It was a hopeless cause.

I was six months pregnant when my mom had warned me not to move in with his mother. "You'll lose him if you move in with her," she prophetically stated.

She was right. It wasn't enough that he was Catholic, Croat Yugoslavian, and sixteen years older than I. According to him, I was also a "Heinz 57" American and a Mormon and wasn't about to join the Catholic church. He had promised before the marriage that I could attend my church when I wanted to. But, when we were married, I was married to his Mother and him, and was expected to do what they wanted me to do.

I was not afforded transportation of any kind, in fear that I may go to my church or escape. When I did refurbish Vince's 25 year old bike and put a child seat in the back and a basket in the front, I was chided about possibly running into trouble with the Mexicans. I needed some way to get groceries while my husband was in the fields.

Having been raised by a very demanding father on our little 20 acre farm in Terra Bella, I was used to taking truck loads of oranges and deliver them to San Francisco, Berkeley, San Jose, and other cities in the Bay area by my self at sixteen years old. I was expected to work like a man, along with my other siblings. My father saw no differences in gender.

I am the oldest of seven children, being born in Porterville, California, to Garlan Eggman and Fidelia Ellen Nelson Eggman. There were seven children born to them. Myself, Teresa Kay, Judith Ellen, Joseph Garlan, Maureen Laura, Suzanne Faye, and Darleen May. I left the house at seventeen, after my Porterville High School graduation in 1970, to go seek my fortune as a secretary in Utah.

After an unsuccessful summer in which I was told to, "Go get married and have a family," by most of the men that interviewed me, I then started to work with my Grandma at the Church Welfare Square in Salt Lake City for food and clothing. It was a good experience for me and I loved living with my Grandma. She was a good example of a woman who never quit. She had gone to school and received her Bachelor's Degree at 57 years old, after she had raised her 10 children. She taught school until she was 72 full-time, and 82 part-time. She was always working for the church at something and going to the Salt Lake City Mormon Temple to do work for her dead every other moment that she could spare. She was an avid Genealogist and inspired myself and my other cousins to do the same.

I dated a young Mormon man named Joe while in Salt Lake City. We would climb Mount Timpanogas, behind Provo, go dune buggying in the soon to be developed housing tracts, go to Liberty Park, where my ancestor, Isaac Chase was once the owner, go to the fun park for all the big rides north of Salt Lake City, and wherever else we could think of. In all, we had a blast. But, I could never feel sexually attracted to this young man. He was more like a brother to me. Indeed, he had the same name as my brother.

After that summer, I knew I needed to go back home to my parents and go to a cheaper college than University of Utah. I knew I couldn't afford such a college. Porterville College was much cheaper.

That's when I met Vince. My father had been selling his grapes because the strike by Cesar Chavez was destroying him and every other grape farmer in California.

Vince would bring his Mexicans to help pack at our house. I was a very fast and efficient packer, having packed ever since I was eleven. The packing machine was place in our carport, next to our house.

It was not hard for me to notice this extremely handsome man with dark hair and eyes at 6 foot 3. I was not used to such an Adonis. I finished out the school year and was married to him in October of 1971. Our daughter Ann Marie, was born July 15, 1972. He went back to his mother in 1973.

After he moved out, he started coming back for sexual favors. It was hard to refuse him. After all, I was still in effect married to him. I told him, "I'm either married to you or not. I did not want to be your mistress!"

Not long after that, a powerful force literally pushed me out of bed early in the morning, and told me to call my dad. Dad and I loaded everything I could on the '49 International pickup, and got out of there like the good 'Okies' that Vince had accused me of being at one time.

Chapter 2

My Ancestory

My Mormon ancestry always intrigued me. Every year, our family would make the trek to Utah for the annual Kennard Reunion. My mom's mother, Teresa Kennard Nelson, was 'grandma' to 42 grandchildren and 110 great-grandchildren when she died. She raised 10 of her eleven children to adulthood, having lost Levi in early childhood.

Levi was named after Levi N. Merrick, a progenitor that had been shot and killed along with his son, Charlie at the Haun's Mill Massacre.

Levi Newton Merrick had trained for the ministry. When he was sent out to preach, he refused to go on with the work, stating he had no authority to do so. He was looking for authority from God and both Philinda and Levi readily accepted to gospel of Jesus Christ of Latter-day Saints.

Shortly after their conversion, Levi had a Patriarchal Blessing. Philinda very seriously voiced with the Patriarch his "Amen" when it was finished.

One statement in the blessing the often pondered over but did not understand was, "You shall be called to preach to the spirits in prison who were rebellious when the long sufferings of the Lord waited in the days of Noah."

In October, 1838, Levi, Philinda and other Saints were journeying from Missouri, from whence that had been driven out to join the saints in Illinois. Indeed, Governor Boggs had signed a law to exterminate all Mormons in Missouri. They stopped at Hauns Mill to rest the Horses. Though assured by the mill owner that it was safe for them to remain there as long as they wished, Brother Merrick felt very uneasy at the tension he sensed all about and resolved to seek out the Prophet Jeseph the next day and learn what was best to do.

The sudden arrival of a mob of 240 well-armed men, left no tomorrow for Brother Merrick.

Philinda Merrick had watched in horror as the men descended upon the mill and proceeded to fire upon all that were inside the mill. Some of the men ran and hid as the mob approached thinking, no doubt, they would not harm women and children. Not so Levi Merrick and a few other intrepid ones. Phililnda witnessed in horror the murder of her husband in cold blood and mortal wounding of her eldest son, Charlie as he lay almost hidden behind the bellows in the blacksmith shop. When the mob had found Charlie, someone stated that he must die, because in their language "nits make lice."

As Levi fell, his distracted wife rushed to him and clasping him in her arms, cried out in anguish of her soul, "Speak to me Levi! Speak to me!"

His voice was stilled, but another voice said to her very distinctly, "You have said, 'Amen.' Let my will, not thine be done." Like a flash, the words of the blessing came to her and she understood their meaning. This knowledge proved a great comfort and strength to her in the trying years that followed.

In the pillaging that was done by the Haun's Mill mob, $700 was taken from Levi Merrick's pocket; proceed from the sale of their former home. The family was now left penniless. Their horses were driven off by the mob.

Hurried burials were necessary and an old dry well was chosen. Among the men who ran away to safety was the father of the Smith boy who was also killed where he was hiding with Charlie Merrick under the bellows. As Brother Merrick's body was being lowered into the well, Smith turned to Philinda and said, "There goes some of your foolhardy bravery."

With flashing eyes, she turned on him with, "I would rather have him lying there than standing in the coward's shoes you stand in."

The doctor who was living in the settlement from whence the mob had come, offered to give help to Charlie Merrick, who was dying from his wounds. Philinda scorned the proffered services saying, "Your kind have done their work, now God and I will take care of him."

To her remaining sons, she would say, "I am always ready to help you unless you come to me with a wound in the back. In that case, I just would not be interested."

Her sons, George and Newton Merrick, later became Pony Express riders for Brigham Young. Abner Eldredge Keeler, a son born to her from her second marriage to Daniel Keeler, became a night watchman for freight trains crossing the plains. He also was a guide and interpreter to the Oregon country and little known trails of the west. All three testified that they were unacquainted with fear.

Most of the survivors of the massacre left the scene as soon as possible, but Philinda Merrick stayed at the mill to care for her wounded son, Charlie, who died the 25th of November, 1838.

Through the help of Brigham Young, she finally reached Nauvoo. Shortly after her arrival in the city, Philinda's father-in-law William Merrick, called on her with the offer to care the family and educate the children if she would denounce Mormonism. She chose to remain with her church and take in sewing to support her family of three; Fanny, Newton and George.

Although a stranger, the Prophet Joseph and his wife Emma, welcomed her as one of the family and provided her with a room in their house where she could support her family with her clever needle. Though penniless, she was rich in a strong testimony of the Gospel and an unwavering will to carry her load.

While living in the Smith Mansion, as the Prophet Joseph's home was known, she helped prepare the curtains for the temple. She also saw the mummies and papyrus from which the "Pearl of Great Price" was translated, as did her daughter Fanny. To her dying day, Fanny did beautiful knitting and was proud to relate how she was taught to knit by the Prophet as she sat on his knee.

One most significant day, Sister Emma came to her room, "Philinda dear," she said, "lay aside your work a minute. I have a message from Joseph. He says the work of the women in the Church is just as important as the work men have to do. He wants to organize us under the power and authority of the Priesthood that we may have the same Heavenly Guidance and direction in our lives the men now have. You have been chosen to be with us at the time. And now I must hurry on, there are many preparations to be made."

Only one who had suffered as Philinda had suffered, first for the lack of that authority and then to be required to give a life of a loved one in payment for receiving the Priesthood of God, could experience the joy it brought to know that she, a woman could have a claim of that authority. Sister Emma's message, unexpected as it was, assured her she no longer need struggle alone, but could be joined in a circle with other women, who under the Priesthood, would be given the authority and power from Heaven for which she had already paid so dearly. Philinda Merrick was one of the Charter members of the Relief Society when it was organized March 17, 1842.

Daniel Hutchison Keeler was working as stone mason on the Nauvoo temple. He and Philinda Merrick were married in 1842. On April 24, 1844, their son, Abner Eldredge, was born. Daniel was born four years later, at St Louis.

During the winter 1845-46, Brother Keeler purchased a new wagon complete in every detail to move his family out of Nauvoo when the call came. Then he went to St. Louis to get money for the trip. In Nauvoo, Philinda's children became ill. She was advised to call in a doctor living nearby. He gave her two doses of colomel. A few days later he presented a bill for $60. Philinda explained Brother Keeler was working in St. Louis and the bill would be paid as soon as he returned. The Doctor threatened to take the case to court. Then he said he would take the new wagon for payment instead. Philinda knew she was helpless to prevent it, so she consented. For this reason, the Keeler family ad to go to St. Louis to get means for the journey to the mountains instead of leaving when the Saints were driven from Nauvoo in 1846.

Somewhere along the way, Philinda was stricken with consumption (as tuberculosis was known in those days). Though, unable to sit up, she decided she must get her family started toward Utah and the body of the Church. In 1859, they left St. Louis in the company under cousin, Horace S. Eldredge. She died en route near Fort Laramie, Wyoming.[1]

The other ancestors that fascinated me were Isaac and Phoebe Chase. Of course, every summer, when our family visited with my mother's family, we went to Liberty Park. We were privileged to be told about this great ancestor who set up the only grist mill in Salt Lake City at the time and 'Mama Chase' would feed and entertain the Saints including Brigham Young, who also married their daughter, Clarisa Chase. (She was one of his reported 51 wives that he had.) Isaac Chase was born on December 12, 1791, in Little Compton, Rhode Island. Phoebe Chase was born on December 7, 1794 in Chenango, Broom County, New York.

Phoebe Ogden first married William Ross in January, 1810 at Cayuga, New York. She separated from him and married Isaac Chase. Three children were born to Phoebe and William Ross. Charles was born December 1810; Theresa was born January 1912; and Clarissa was born June 8, 1813.

Six children were born to Phoebe Ogden Ross and Isaac Chase. Sylvia was born August 4, 1819; Desdamona on April 3, 1821; Maria on April 5, 1826; Rhoda on September 39, 1830; George Ogden on March 11, 1832; and Harriet Louisa on April 28, 1834.

In the year 1840, Isaac and Phoebe Chase and their family, (except Charles and Theresa) were converted to The Church of Jesus Christ of Latter-day Saints. They were baptized by Peletiah Brown at Sparta, Livingston County, New York.

Isaac Chase was a miller. They lived in a large frame house surrounded by sugar maples, where they were comfortably settled for life. After accepting the gospel, the sold their farm at a sacrifice and moved to Nauvoo, Illinois. There were six to eight wagons in the company. People flocked to see such a marvelous sight and were doubly surprised to see they were Mormons.

---

1 Excerpts from history of Philinda Eldridge Merrick Keeler written by her granddaughter, Philinda Keeler Naelge.

Isaac Chase bought a farm three miles out of Nauvoo on the Mississippi River. His brother Ezra, also one of the parties who had come from New York and Isaac were attending a meeting shortly after their arrival, when someone spoke in tongues. The interpretation was given in the way of advice to the brothers to return to New York and dispose of all their holdings for money to donate to the Church in its financial crisis. They were given a portion of merchandise in the Nauvoo Store. The two younger children of Isaac and Phoebe were baptized by the Prophet Joseph in the Mississippi River when George was ten and Louisa eight. Isaac and Phoebe were sealed in the Nauvoo Temple on December 13, 1845, as husband and wife, where they worked day and night.

During the epidemic of winter fever, their daughter, Sylvia, was stricken. She was very sick and they sent for the Prophet to come and administer to her, but he was so busy with other sick people that he was unable to go. He sent he handkerchief and told her to hold it, and it would be the same as a blessing. This she did, and her fever left her, and she began to get well immediately.

Phoebe Chase was also a member of the firsts Relief Society of the Church, though not present on the day it was organized by Joseph Smith. She was set apart and ordained into the priesthood of God (women are not now ordained in the Mormon Church) by the prophet to administer to the sick. She had the gift of healing sealed upon her. She was very faithful in this gift of healing sealed upon her. She was very faithful in this calling, and many seemingly miraculous healings resulted. At one time, her husband, Isaac, was so ill, his life was despaired of. She went out under the trees alone and prayed for him; and a few moments, he began to get better and soon recovered.

At this time, Clarissa Chase and her friend, Ellen Rockwood, were married at the same time to Brigham Young. This took place at the time of the persecution of the Prophet. Often, there were 12 men of the guard. Beds were all over the floor as they tried to catch a wink of sleep. At the slightest noise, they were up and out.

This condition existed until Joseph and Hyrum were taken to Carthage and martyred. It was intimate and personally heartbreaking to the Chase family to have Joseph and Hyrum martyred. They had been so close to the Prophet and loved him so sincerely. But like so many others, the things of the moment were so pressing and important for the membership of the Church that their attention had to be given to plans for the great exodus of the Saints from Nauvoo. Isaac and Phoebe, with other members of the Chase family, left Nauvoo, crossed the Mississippi River and made their way to Winter Quarters. There, Isaac dug a hole in the ground, covered it and built steps down into it. The family lived there all winter. They had a cow; they had purchased two barrels full of corn, which the ground as needed; and that was their principal item of food.

After leaving Winter Quarters in June of 1847, they were in Jedediah M. Grant's Hundred, Bates Noble's Fifty and Robert Pierce's Ten. They were soon away from all the settlements and on a vast prairie among the Indians and buffalo. Once, a stampede of buffalo came so close to the camp, the ground trembled. A number of the men went out on horses and fired guns and pistols and with difficulty, turned them aside. At another time, their oxen stampeded because a rider flapped a buffalo robe and frightened the m. They were near a deep ravine, wondering how best to cross, when the oxen took to their heads and plunged through the gully. One broken wagon was the only accident.[2]

John S. Gleason had been reported to be the first person to destroy the press in Nauvoo that Joseph commanded him to destroy. He was also in the Carthage Jail with Joseph and Hyrum when asked to go home because he was carrying too many guns. The next day, Joseph and Hyrum were murdered by the mob. John S. Gleason was one of the scouting parties that preceded Brigham Young's camp into the Salt Lake Valley on July 22, 1847. He prepared the Valley along with others for the Saints arrival. In August, he returned to Winter Quarters. He brought his family to Salt Lake the following summer. He had married Desdemona Chase, daughter of Isaac and Phoebe Chase. Their first child was born at Elkhorn on their way to Salt Lake. They named him Alvirus. A second son born in Salt Lake died at the age of four years. Their third child and first daughter was born in St. John while he was working a mining claim in Tooele County in 1852—Joanna Louisa—always called "Sis."

The Gleasons had taken a contract out to cook for the men who were building the railroad through Weber Canyon, and Sis went along to help. Leonidas Hamlin Kennard, a Civil War Veteran and a great-great grandson of a Revolutionary Soldier, began to noticed Sis. He soon asked John for Sis's hand in marriage. He said, "If you were a member of the Church, I wouldn't hesitate"; but the suitor was too honest to "buy" his bride thus. The Parents gave their consent, however; and on the groom's birthday, they were married by her father in the Stoddard home, where they first met.

They had thirteen children, eleven of whom grew to maturity. All were born in Farmington. Leonidas taught school, was Post Master, storekeeper, blacksmith, and staunch member of the Church, which he joined to the fall after his first child was born, being baptized by Father Gleason, who had never despaired of teaching him the Gospel. The child was very sick and the Elders were called to give him a blessing in which the child soon thereafter recovered. This is when he decided to join the Church.[3]

My Grandma, Teresa Kennard Nelson, was one of his thirteen children.

---

[2] Excerpts taken from Leonidas Hamlin Kennard II, His Family.
[3] Ibid, Vol. I & II

Her fiery red hair and temperance to go with it, attracted Virgil H. Nelson, son of a Swedish immigrant that had accepted the Gospel of Jesus Christ in Sweden and had moved to Salt Lake City and met a granddaughter of Philinda Merrick Keeler named Fidelia. My mother, her namesake was one of the eleven children born to Teresa Kennard Nelson and Virgil H. Nelson.

Her namesake was my mother, Fidelia Ellen Nelson Eggman. Mom was past her prime at 21 or 22 when she was called by Church to serve a mission to Mexico during the war to be a secretary to the Mission President in Mexico City. She had served in Washington D.C. for the Defense Secretary as a secretary for his office for a time after she had put herself through Latter-day Saint Business College correcting English papers for two bits an hour. She took the college exam for English in Utah State University and literally blew the top off the exam.

She then put in an application for teaching school in Tooele. This is where she met my father, an ex-Navy man in World War II, that was on the USS Enterprise during the bombing of Pearl Harbor, through a mutual friend by the name of Jeanie Blackburn. They began corresponding, and he kept on saying, "I'm coming out," meaning he was coming to marry her. She was getting interested in a man named Long John, and told my father to forget coming out. Almost the very next day, he was out to Tooele, slipped a ring on my maiden mother's hand, and immediately asked her to marry him. She was attracted to him because he did not mince words and definitely did not waste any time in letting her know his intentions. She was 27 and he was 30 when they were married ten days later in the Salt Lake Temple.

Coming from a completely different background than Mom, Garlan Eggman was a convert to the Church. His Cherokee Indian/Irish mother, Judith Fears, was a product of her Cherokee Indian mother, Mary Eeds, and Irish father. They were not married at the time. It was a Cherokee tradition that a woman could pick the man they wanted to have children by and it was considered common-law. She had two sets of twins by Mr. Fears, only my Uncle Clyde and Judith lived to adulthood. Judith Fears, or Mom-Judy, as she liked being called, relayed to me that she was married off like a sack of potatoes to 'Old man Eggman' when she was fifteen. Her mother's boyfriend was beginning to be attracted to her, and her mother wouldn't have it. Arthur Eggman was a very handsome German that happened to notice Judith. They had seven children; Garlan, Eugene, Ardith, Arthur Clyde, Andrew Max, Shirley Ray, and Barbara Muriel. She was despairing that after five boys, that the next was to be named Shirley Ray, whether the child was a boy or a girl. It was a boy. It smacks kind of like the boy named 'Sue.' They had come in from the dust bowl of the '30's during the depression to be fruit tramps in California. They happened to be living in Hoover's Camp in Bakersfield while the 'Grapes of Wrath' was being filmed there.

After much hardship through Arthur's hard drinking and gambling ways and losing everything he would own, the family finally settled in Terra Bella. They became big apiary (bee)farmers in which some of my dad's brothers still do.

Garlan joined the church because of a "bum" that he had befriended told him that if there were a church that he would join, it would be the Mormon Church. Coming from where he was, he finally stumbled into a testimony meeting one Sunday in the Church of Jesus Christ of Latter-day Saints. After listening to the testimonies of the Saints, he got up and bore his testimony. He was filled with the spirit and stated that this was the true Church. He later found out that this was the Mormon Church and joined. He was an avid missionary all his life, handing out Books of Mormon in every language he could find. He even gave Mikael Gorbachev, the Russian President, five Russian Books of Mormon, along with five boxes of oranges while the President was at the Presidio in San Francisco. He often stated that was one of the reasons why the Berlin Wall came down. For a fact, it was not long after his gift that the wall did come down.

It was not hard to catch my father's zeal from his testimony of the Book of Mormon. When I finally read it and put its promise to the test, the Holy Spirit revealed to me that it was a true book of God. It was a record of my Indian Ancestors of which I was very proud and happy to read about. It was about God loving people even in this continent and taking the time to come these people after his resurrection because of their great love for him. I found that God is no respecter of persons and will come to anyone who loves him with this book.[4]

---

[4] My own personal recollections of what my father and mother has related to me.

Chapter 3

Post Divorce

When Joe had come back from his mission, I had already been married and divorced with my little daughter, Ann. I looked him up and he seemed to take it all in stride. He came out to California to live in an apartment in Porterville, so we could be closer together. He got a job and brought his boat. We would go skiing up at Lake Success above Porterville. I could never get the hang of water skiing, but my sister Teresa did. I started to see that he was getting to be attracted to her. Why not, she was single, never had given him a 'Dear John' while on his mission, and did not come with baggage. We had a great summer in which I gave him my ring for my size finger. He promptly 'lost' the ring. He then gave me a large marquis engagement ring, that my sister Judy lost in the park.

When I went to Kanab to visit him, he was so engrossed in helping his mother around her house, he seemed to forget about me. Ann seemed to like him, but I did not need another mama's boy. I had to pay my way back to California, after he promised he would, and then broke up with him.

The next return missionary I dated was Rick. He was the "Golden Boy" of the return missionaries. He was taken around to all the Wards of the Stake and touted as the "Catch of the Church," for all of us young ladies interested. I was interested.

Rick, was fairly handsome, six foot four and had a good job as an assistant accountant. He made more money than I did at Montgomery Wards for $2.75 an hour. He was attending Fresno State and was a champion basketball player while in high school. Indeed, he showed me scrapbook after scrapbook of his high school jumping abilities. He was considered the highest jumper in the region. I could tell he was very proud of his accomplishments. When I asked where his mother was, he stated that she was in a mental institution.

He then began counting my money from my divorce with his money to pay his bills. Of course, being the future 'good Mormon wife' in following the 'priesthood' that I was taught all my life that it was my duty to do as the female member of the Church, I went along with it – for a while. He bought new tires for his car, while my tires were bald. Indeed, my poor '64 Chevy 'Red Bomb' as I called it, the Bel Air could barely make it to Porterville and back without overheating. I could barely pay rent, let alone buy food for my daughter and me. Then he started coming to my apartment at all hours of the night. My non-Mormon friends started talking. When I told him this fact, he said, "So, let them talk. It's our business what we do."

When Mom and Dad offered us their mobile home, he jumped at the chance, and wanted more. Mom and Dad started hinting that I better watch this young man because he appeared to be a Gigolo and was out to get whatever he could.

The final straw came when he ripped all the pictures of Vince and me and Annie up while I dutifully helped him. I had carefully taken them out of my albums to keep them out my sight, and he had discovered them and demanded that they be ripped up, so I wouldn't be tempted to live in the past.

I cried for two weeks.

I broke up with him, to my money back from him by threatening to go to his bishop and tell him what he did, and then vowed never to date a Mormon return missionary again.

My mother then warned me, watch out for men. They like to date divorced women, because they were easy targets for sex.

"Aw Mom," I answered, "that won't happen to me. I'll be careful."

I soon found out differently. It was refreshing to date non-Mormons again. Of course, they had no scruples and no morals. My Catholic-Jew was even a more fantastic love than my husband was. That relationship came to a screeching halt when my father bashed in his Volkswagon van's front windows and would have done him in if I hadn't stepped between them. I found out the hard way why my husband had let me know he wouldn't have married me if it hadn't been for my dad.

Then, I found out why my mother warned me against dating Hispanic men. They think nothing of molesting and raping a woman. That ended when I told him I would call the cops on him after I found out I was pregnant and even went to the clinic for an abortion only to find out that all my other efforts to kill the baby inside me worked. I wasn't about to have a baby that the father wasn't going to marry me and had not intentions of doing so.

Of course, I had to confess all my sins to the Bishop. He kept a close eye on me. When I wanted to go to BYU, after going straight, he was rather skeptical, but finally approved. You have to be a "good" Latter-day Saint to go to BYU. This was the year of 1975.

It was always our habit as a family to start our trek to Utah in the evening to beat the heat of the desert. After loading y daughter and securing her, we were off to Provo. Leaving the orchard and vineyards of California and driving through the hot desert night with the full moon was peaceful. Annie slept through the night drive and we arrived in Provo the next day.

Provo, that beautiful town, nestled beneath the towering Wasatch Mountains and under Mount Timpanogos, the same one I hiked with Joe not too long before. Provo is the epitome of a perfect Mormon town. Every street is perfectly straight with number of South, North, East and West put perfectly on a grid according Brigham Youngs' design of a perfect Zionic city.

The address given to me by my old church dance partner, Randy, was soon found. Randy and his wife, Teryl, were very helpful in hooking me up with their landlord. Ann and I stayed with them on the floor and couch that night.

The next day, Kyle came over after I called him. He proceeded to show me some more of his houses he was maintaining for his brothers. Each person paid for their room and board. So, if there were three to four girls sharing a bedroom in a three bedroom house, the owners stood to be making a tidy sum of money. I didn't want to share a bedroom with young women that had never been married and did not have children. It made me feel awkward. I asked Kyle if he had a studio apartment any where with a back yard.

"Yes," he replied, and had Annie and I follow him up the street from where Randy and his new bride were staying. He stopped in front of a modest, white-framed home. It was different from the other brick homes on the block. We walked around the two strips of concrete for a driveway and went around the back to a set of stairs going down to a door below the back of the house. He opened it, and there painted in fairly fresh lime-green paint was the tiny studio apartment. It had an old-fashioned steel sink with a wash side to put your drying dishes, a small bathroom with a shower, a small apartment gas stove, a fridge, and barely a place for a couch-bed, table, a couple of chairs, and perhaps a piano.

It had a beautiful sunken back yard with a large swaying willow tree in the back part of the yard. This was the perfect place for Annie and I.

"I don't have much money, and I still have to pay for my books and food. How much do you want per month for this place?" I inquired.

"I'm asking sixty a month for it." Kyle politely replied.

"I can give you forty a month. That is all I can afford," I counteroffered.

"That will be fine," he answered after a pause, "after all, people are more important than houses."

This man intrigued me. He was definitely not the tall, dark, and handsome type of man as Vince was, but he was about six foot, had the broadest shoulders I had ever seen on any man, hazel eyes, reddish blond hair, and quite handsome with his reddish mustache.

"Is there any way that I can get some furniture such as a couch-bed for this apartment?" I inquired.

"I'll have Vic bring one over right now," he replied. With that, he promptly called Vic, and the couch was delivered within the hour.

I then inquired if he had a piano and a table and some chairs. He then proceeded to deliver them as promptly as I requested them.

I then procured a sweet Mormon lady for a babysitter on the corner. She was taking in babysitting while her husband was attending college.

With that, I went to explore the campus, procure my books I would be needing for my Botany class, Book of Mormon class, and Piano class. I also took a ball room dancing class. The burgundy-red journal that I bought was so handsome, I delighted to write in it.

Chapter 4

First Choice

July 6, Sunday 1975
Dear Journal,

Today I went to hear the new General Authority that took over Elder Hunter's place at the Marriott Center at BYU. His wonderful speech was about the freedoms of this country. Then he went to free agency. We have studied free agency in my Book of Mormon class and I'm just now beginning to catch a glimpse of what it really means.

From what I understand, free agency is the very thing that Jesus stood for. You must have the freedom to choose right from wrong in all things if you are to grow and develop in the gospel and your life. 2 Nephi 2:27 is a good example of this. It says, "…men are that they might have joy."

Apparently, the more wrong choices I make in my life, the less free agency I will have. I just hope I haven't blown it too much.

Tonight, as I was talking and reading the Bible to Annie, I was amazed at how much she comprehended about Jesus and how simple and pure her conclusions were.

I was reading to her about the parable of the sower and told her Jesus was saying these things to his disciples. Instantly, she knew who I was talking about and our conversation about Jesus left tears in my eyes.

She said, "Jesus is in the sky. I want him to come to my house and see me. I will give him ice cream and some cheetos."

Her innocence in her statement was very poignant. "Jesus will come again," I explained, and he is a man like your Daddy."

The phrase often struck me what Christ once said, "Except ye are as little children, ye cannot enter into the kingdom of heaven."[5]

I didn't really understand many of the wonders of the world, or I had forgotten them, and I began to see the wonders of the world through the eyes of my child. Things began to change around me. Watching a bug as it crawled on the ground with her was whole new world or water going along the road and putting our feet in front of it to stop it, put power in her and I. Children look at everything as wondrous and either good or bad; no gray in the middle.

With that in mind, she and I snuggled the best we could on the couch bed with all its lumps and valleys.

Chapter 5
"Three"

Wednesday, July 15, 1975
Dear Journal,

Today was Annie's birthday. I wasn't able to give her a party today. I was too busy going to dance class and meeting this guy from Florida. His father has five acres of oranges, so we had something in common. He didn't seem bothered at all that I had a little girl and wanted her to come, too.

The first night I went to my dance class, I had Annie with me. I was walking toward my car and he offered us a ride. The second night of dancing, we did not have much of a chance to meet each other. Last Wednesday, I brought my car and he surprised me by asking me for a ride home.

"Did you bring our car?" he asked inquiringly.

Not knowing what he meant by 'our' car, I reluctantly replied, "Yes."

"Good!" he retorted. "My car's water pump is broken."

Neither of knew what our majors were, but promised each other we would find out by the end of the summer.

Thursday, July 16
Dear Journal,

Today, I was able to give Annie her birthday party. After I signed up for my classes, and secure an apartment, I was ready to give my daughter a nice party. She had managed to make friends with her babysitter's children, plus a few other children at church.

I asked her what kind of cake she wanted. She answered, "I want a round cake with frosting on it."

I bought balloons for her and a present. The children had a wonderful time playing in the back yard under the swaying willow tree. Annie loved her presents and party. That night, I thanked the Lord for our happiness and blessings.

Wednesday, July 24
Dear Journal,

It has been a week and a half since I wrote, so I thought I would do a little catching up. First of all, I think I'll start from the beginning of my coming here before I get into my story.

I did talk about my landlord and mentioned that he was a wonderful person and God will bless him, but, I thought it inconsequential that he invited me out for ice cream – twice. Once, about the first time we met, and the other a little later. It seemed as if ice cream was the favorite past time of Provo, Utah since drinking was not what Mormons did. I suppose the spur of the moment way it happened is what didn't phase me. Also, he was still infatuated with this girl named Nola that he had dated before.

After those inconsequential happenings, I thought I may as well invite him to a picnic that a girlfriend of mine and her boyfriend had invited Annie and myself to. I called him two hours before we went, which isn't very much time to prepare, but, I really didn't want to be the third party (three's a crowd.) Since Kyle was the only man I knew the telephone number of, I called and invited him.

He came back with an immediate, "Yes!"

Of course, the quickness of his answer surprised me. How many people can you invite on the spur of the moment that probably will come up with a hundred excuses for not going?

"I'll explain later why I answered so quickly under the shade of a tree," he explained.

We had a wonderful time. He ended up telling me at Kentucky Fried Chicken. "I was on my knees praying to the Lord on what to do next, when you called and invited me," he explained. "I felt that your call was the answer to my prayer."

While I pondered on what he told me, we traveled up to Provo Canyon. The summer canyon was exploding with the Bridal Veil Falls, the lush greenery, the pines, the river running through it, and the lush undergrowth. It was much like Logan canyon, the one our family would visit every summer for our Kennard Family Reunions.

The other guy that was dating my friend made a statement to Kyle, "Doesn't she have a beautiful smile?"

"Yes," Kyle answered, "with sensuous lips."

Kyle's answer kind of surprised me.

I had been praying about what to do about going back and marrying

Vince. About two days after this picnic, (approximately two to three weeks after I arrived in Provo, which was June the 19th, 1975, I received an answer to my prayers. I was washing the dishes at the time and the Lord, in a very loud voice said, "Kyle is going to be your next husband!"

I was so shocked and astounded with this very loud voice from the Lord, I exclaimed out loud – "No Way!!! This can't be!! . . . . I don't love him! , , , , ,I still love my first husband . . . Kyle is just a friend! . . .I don't want to marry him!" . . . . and other explanations I argued with the Lord. But, I knew it was futile arguing with him,

He was the last person I would have chosen for a husband, no matter how nice he is to Annie and me!

Of course, the voice didn't answer back to my arguments, but I knew from whence it came. I knew what the answer to my prayers was even if I wasn't happy with them.

I always had the goal of getting married in the Mormon Temple ever since I was a little girl. Vince, no matter how much I wanted it, fell on deaf ears. What did I expect? I realized he broke his promises he made to me before he married me that he would take me to my church if I would go to his. It got real one-sided after we married. "You now belong to me, and I don't have to do anything I promised before we were married," he factually stated one day, when I asked about his promises.

This put a new meaning to double standard to me.

He was angry when I went to my church, I had to be picked up because of lack of transportation he made sure I didn't have. Having the Home Teachers and Visiting Teachers over were grounds for not speaking for four months, after which he asked for a divorce. It didn't matter that he was very unhappy with the Catholic Church for supporting Cesar Chavez in the grape boycott which almost did him and all the other Catholic grape growers in. If it hadn't been for my Dad selling the fully packed grapes for wine, the family would have gone completely under and lost everything.

I had prayed mightily that Vince would change his mind and join the Church and take me to the temple, for I did love him so, but, to no avail.

I then had a dream that him and I were standing in a line in heaven waiting for our pillows. When we got to the gate, we were told there were no pillows because they weren't needed in heaven.

"Oh, Lord," I pleaded, "Why do you want me to marry Kyle? What am I going to tell Vince?" All these things and many more went round and round in my head until I was almost dizzy. The voice didn't answer back to my arguments, but I knew from whence it came and I knew what my answer to my prayers was even if I wasn't happy with them.

I wrote to my parents about how things were going. I told them about my landlord, whom seemed to be a nice friend. They promptly wrote back in separate letters to stay away from my landlord! They then gave me parental advice to come back and marry Vince. They also sent me some much needed money.

What was I going to tell them about this very loud voice from God telling me to marry Kyle? I for sure didn't want to tell them anything about it, especially after my patriarchal blessing had stated to listen to my parents, and they would direct me in the right path.

I dropped out of dancing class because of Kyle's suggestion.

There was a guy that asked me out for Wednesday, July 16th. I had only a total of nine hours of sleep for the two days and put on the birthday party for Annie. I felt very tired and the spirit wasn't right about going out with him, so I cancelled the date.

I wanted to go to the Mormon Pageant in Manti and I was told in the spirit to ask Kyle again. I thought I would be forward asking the same person to go some place with me. I felt a little awkward about calling him and asking him for a date. After all, society did not operate in that manner. I was always taught this was a man's place.

Again, he accepted readily. The couple that lived in the front of the house where my basement apartment was had mentioned that Kyle and I made a cute couple and perhaps we should get married. Of course, at the time, I flatly denied any feelings for Kyle.

He came back with, "I don't think you and Annie would make a bad family at all." He then proceeded to list the reasons why.

Chapter 6
Kyle's Entry – Proposal

July 23, 1975;

I guess I should set down the events of the last few weeks so that they won't be forgotten. Tuesday, 19; A. Carla phoned me about living at 684 North, 400 East. From that address, she had looked at it and kind of wanted it and then explained about her situation. I suggested 772 East, rear basement, and she asked, "How's $40?"

I said, "Yes, and explained that people were the most important consideration. She had come over and was there. We signed contracts. I took $52 from her; $12 for the rest of June and a $40 deposit.

Tuesday, July 1. She came over when I was talking to Voyne (my maintenance man.) She was patient as I talked and waited even after I had written out a receipt for her rent. I felt that I should do something and invited her out for ice cream. Sometime in the week following, I went over to see how she was okay and see if Voyne had gotten the bed for her.

Saturday, July 6. I stopped on my way home from work before my way to my interview to become an Elder. I did not stay long.

Monday, July 8. After being ordained an Elder on Sunday, I stopped by to say "Hello," and you fed me chicken. You told me about stopping by my place earlier to invite me to dinner and I wasn't home. I returned the money I had borrowed from you when we went for ice cream. (End of Kyle's entry.)

I wrestled with my dilemma of God's voice talking to me for two weeks, keeping up a front to Kyle. He was the only friend I had in Provo that I felt comfortable enough to talk to in Provo. We got to know each other better on a friendship basis only. I could not really see going any further with this man. Especially to marry him.

He proved to be a very good friend to Annie and I. He came to talk about subject on the gospel of Jesus Christ and other things in life. His philosophies of life and eternal progression were astounding to me. I never met anyone as deep thinking in the gospel as he was. The more I got to know him, the more I could see that he was a very good man . . . but, not to marry. "Why me Lord?" I kept on asking myself.

Then, Vince wrote me a letter. He told me how much he loved me and missed me. The letter was the most sincere letter I had ever received from anyone. I couldn't take the torment any longer! I had to tell Kyle what was going on.

"Kyle, Sit down," I commanded nicely. He sat down on the couch bed he had supplied for my little apartment. "There is something I have to tell you that I don't quite know what to do about."

I took a long pause while he patiently waited. "The Lord has told me that you are going to be my next husband."

There was a long, awkward silence as I let him digest what I had just told him. I sighed a very heavy sigh and went on. "I had promised my first husband that I would go back and marry him after this summer of attending BYU, but it looks like the Lord wants things to go very differently than what I had planned. What do you think about all of what I'm saying?"

Kyle sat there looking at me calmly, digesting what I had just laid on him and probably mulling through his mind for an answer. I was surprised he didn't bolt for the door right then and there. Any other man probably would have.

After a very long pause, he said, "What do you want to do?"

"I want to do what the Lord has told me to do, in spite of my other wishes. What do you think about all this?" I repeated.

"I have had a similar voice come to me and tell me that I was to marry you, but I didn't want to say anything about it, because we haven't even come close to the subject. I also figured that we were just good friends and no more would come of our friendship. Do you think you could marry me based on our friendship and the Lord telling you to marry me?" was Kyle's reply.

"I don't know, Kyle," I said plaintively, this is pretty heavy duty stuff we're discussing. Why don't we pray about it?"

We then proceeded to kneel down around the piano bench he had provided for me along with the piano and prayed. I had never prayed with my first husband so this was a first. Our prayers were very earnest indeed. This was an intense moment for both of us and we were both a little shaky. When we were finished, a strong feeling rushed over both of us as we looked each other in the eye. I knew what I had to do.

"What shall I tell Vince?" I very softly and furtively asked Kyle.

"He wrote me a letter a few days ago about how much he loved me and is waiting for Ann and I to come back and get married."

"Let me see the letter," said Kyle very businesslike. He quickly read and analyzed the letter then turned to me and asked, "Would he ever join this Church?"

"No," was my very positive answer.

"Would he ever take you to the temple and be married for eternity?" was his next question.

"No," had to be my answer again.

"Will he ever have any respect for your beliefs?"

My answer had to be negative once more. It was painful to have to be so honest and really look at the reality of the situation.

"Then, it goes to show you, Carla, that you would be getting into the same mess you were in before, no matter how much you love or loved him," he stated calmly and very matter of fact way. "Why would you want to go back to the same thing, knowing all this to be true?"

I knew at the bottom of my heart he was speaking the truth and it broke it even more. Kyle could sense this deep sorrow in my heart and gave me a hug. Then he said, "Do you ever think that you could love and marry a friend?"

Almost in tears, I replied, "If you can understand where I am coming from and know of the love I have and had for Vince, then I can marry a friend."

Hopefully, love will come later, I thought to myself. This was definitely different from the deep longing and love that I had felt for Vince. I wasn't sure what to think or to expect.

Vince found out about my marriage when he called my parents at the end of the summer to see if I was at my parents' house. They had the dubious duty of telling him that I was on my honeymoon.

When Kyle left that night, he said, "I'm scared."

I knew why he said this statement, so it didn't surprise me when he came back the next day and said, "I think I should marry you," in a very matter of fact way.

Of course, I was already expecting the proposal.

We then kissed and hugged each other.

On Saturday, July 19, we went to Salt Lake City to turn over some papers to a war game which Kyle had been playing and then went to my Grandma Nelson's house. While we were waiting for her to return from the temple which she attended faithfully, I showed Kyle all of her pictures of our families. My wedding picture to Vince was also in the albums. I pointed it out to Kyle. He remarked, "You were a very pretty bride."

Since we were so new with the idea of getting married, I just introduced him as my friend so I wouldn't create a commotion. My Uncle Grant and Aunt Maureen were there for our family reunion. Uncle Grant told me that he liked Kyle. This made me feel good because I respected his opinion. When Grandma came back from the temple, after talking to him, she like him. It was very comforting to know that the person I was going to marry was liked by the people I loved and admired.

We went over to my Uncle Nels' house and had bar-b-cued steak. It was fun to be around all of my relatives whom I knew and loved. Ann had a great time playing with all of her cousins.

We then returned back to Provo. Ann and I went back to our green basement after a hug and a kiss from Kyle, and he went back to his apartment.

Kyle decided that he should spend more time with me, so he went to church with Ann and me. We had a wonderful time together. It was so very nice to be able to sit in my church with a man that practiced the same religion and believed the same way I did. Kyle was a good singer and I enjoyed singing with him. He put his arm around me. I seemed so natural. Ann seemed to be happy with the arrangement, also.

We returned to Sacrament meeting and Ann woke up from a nap and screamed for forty-five minutes. We took her to the nursery room. Kyle was very patient with her. I really feel that she has had to make a lot of adjustments from having Mommy all to herself to having to share me.

I'm also finding that Kyle is wonderful in giving me the encouragement and backing I need to raise her. It's so much easier to have someone help with the raising of the children.

I went for food stamps today. I would be getting $94 worth of food for $18. It's so tempting, but I kind of feel wrong about it. I was not raised to ask the government to help with food or anything else. As long as I could work, I would work. Kyle suggested that I go to the Bishop and ask where my home teachers are and maybe ask him about getting help.

Chapter 7

Out Loud

Sunday, July 27, 1975
Dear Journal,

Kyle, Ann and I went to see Bishop Blackham and went to his Ward for Sunday school. Kyle talked first. He told him about us from the beginning to the present. Sitting there listening, I found out many things about Kyle that he hadn't told me. So, I found it very interesting to just listen.

He explained that he had been on his knees praying one day as to what he should do next, when I called him for the picnic. After we had both discussed things with the Bishop and left his office, I felt such a spiritual high. I had never felt this way before when I was with other young men that I was thinking of marrying.

After leaving his office, we then went to Provo to visit Kyle's Grandma Hatch. This was the only close family had around at this time as his family were all in Panama at this time. She lived in a rest home in Provo. I really got to know and love this very spry and smart woman. She reminded me of my Grandma Nelson.

After the visit, I had to get busy and write a letter to Bishop Christenson, my former Bishop in Porterville that had given me permission to attend BYU as long as I behaved myself. While I was concentrating on the letter, Kyle came barging in and startled me. Jumping a little, I said, "I didn't know you were here, and you surprised me."

He grabbed the letter and read it. "I don't like the letter, it doesn't sound very good. But if you feel that it is right to send it, then do it," he stated with a flat affect.

Not knowing what to expect and surprise and a little hurt at what he said, I cried. I suppose from all of the things that had been happening, I was so emotional that crying came very easily at this time. I took a little while for us to come to an agreement as to why I reacted the way I did, but after a while of him making sure I was honest about my feelings we straightened things out.

I then confided in him about things which I had never even thought of before. He asked if I prayed out loud to the Lord. I answered, "No." I explained to him that some friends had told me that if I do, Satan would hear me and get the greater advantage over me.

"When you pray out loud," he explained, "you defy Satan and tell him out loud you are not afraid of him. Satan loves people to pray in secret because it gives him power over you. You aren't able to say complete sentences in your head and don't make any sense. You can't get the depth of your request to the Lord that you would have if you don't pray aloud."

"Satan also works through your friends," he added. "If he can't drag you down through your friends, he will outright confront you in other ways."

This gave me much to ponder about. I had never had anyone talk to me as powerfully as he did on the subject of Satan. It was almost as though he had a personal knowledge of him.

Tuesday, July 29, 1975
Dear Journal,
Today, I was reading in the Book of Mormon in Mosiah 2:21-29 and Mosiah 3:19. In the first reference it says,

". . . . If ye should serve him who has created you from the beginning, and is preserving you from day to day, by lending you breath, that ye may live and move and do according to your own will, and even supporting you from one moment to another, I say, if ye should serve him with all our souls yet ye would be unprofitable servants.

. . . .behold, all that he requires of you is to keep his commandments; and he promised you that if ye would keep his commandments, ye should prosper in the land; and he never doth vary from that which he hath said; therefore if ye do keep his commandments, he doth bless you and prosper you . . ."

These scriptures really brought to my mind the eternal indebtedness that I had to my God. I will apply this to my life. When I lived contrary to the laws of God, I suffered. Right now, I'm living God's commandments and the blessings that I am feeling are almost beyond my capacity to bear them. I must always remember the great debt I owe him and humble myself before my God.

The other scripture is; ". . . for natural man is an enemy to God and has been from the fall of Adam, and will be forever and ever, unless he yields to the enticing of the Holy Spirit, and puts off the natural man and becomes a Saint through the atonement of Christ the Lord, and becomes as a child, submissive, willing to submit to all things which the Lord sees fit to inflict upon him, even as a child doth submit to his father."

This scripture also is important to me now as I am waiting to marry Kyle. I must remember to be submissive to the Holy Spirit. It is difficult to wait for the glorious day to happen.

Kyle announced to me today that we were getting married September 1st. This announcement made me very happy. I feel we shouldn't wait much longer than this date. I was also worried about whether I would receive my Temple Recommend in that short of time. Kyle reassured me that if the Lord willed that we were to get married in the temple, He will find the way to make it happen.

It was hard for me to have the same kind of faith that Kyle seemed to have. It was something I seemed to need to build. The thought then came to me that Vince might sue for custody of Ann when he found out about my marriage to Kyle. But, a good feeling came to me from the Holy Spirit not to worry about it at this time.

I then felt I needed to inform my parents about what was happening to me, so I wrote a letter to them.

July 29, 1975
Dear Mom and Dad,

I'm writing to you what I feel most necessary in my heart to tell you. This is one of the most difficult letters that I have ever written. Much prayer and though has gone into what I'm about to write to you. I feel that while I'm writing to you the Holy Spirit is with me and I hope and pray that He will also be with you as you read this letter.

What I have to tell you is that I'm getting married to Kyle approximately September 1st. We have known about this for two weeks. We plan on a temple marriage in the Manti Temple when I receive my recommend.

The reason I have been hesitant about telling you is that I remember both of you distinctly cautioning me against being even friendly with my landlord. Now my future husband is my landlord at the present time.

I sincerely tried to follow your counsel, for it was very wise counsel, but the Lord just seemed to have other things in mind for me.

I had been praying for many years for the Lord to tell me whom to marry. None of the other men I've gone with had answers from the Lord, not even the return missionaries.

Well, the answer came very loud and clear that I was to marry Kyle even before I had any idea of liking him as a friend. I've never felt so right about anything in my life.

I also figured out that my Patriarchal blessing meant that when I was older and more mature, it would be my responsibility to find a companion. One who lives right, one who is clean, and one who holds the priesthood so he and I can go to the temple and there be married and sealed for time and eternity.

I feel that the time is now, and I was mainly responsible for what is happening. I feel that I have accomplished that part in my blessing in what it said about after going to school to consult my parents and do what they tell me, no matter what the calling was.

I feel that I fulfilled this in marrying Vince. There must've been a wise and glorious purpose in it, but as to right now, I know not what.

As for a companion for eternal life, I feel at this time that I couldn't ask for a more righteous man than Kyle. He lives right, is clean, and holds the priesthood. The greatest consideration that I have at this time is that I am learning to love him dearly. I feel, without a doubt, he fully qualified to make an excellent husband for me and a good father for Ann.

My schooling is not in any way lacking because of what is happening. Instead, I am doing better in school. However, I am not going to school next semester or the next. I am doing as you suggested, Dad, to settle down, get married and raise a family.

I can feel no better time than in the near future than to accomplish this.

Ann is doing fine. She loves it here in Provo with all her little friends. We had a wonderful birthday party for her.

I feel that I have written enough to inform you about Ann and myself. I hope you well feel the spirit in which I have written to you.

> I say these things
> Sincerely and lovingly,
> Carla and Ann

Chapter 8

Past Histories

Dear Journal,

I had a very long conversation with Kyle tonight about our past histories. I really feel that one must know the other person, bad or good, and part of that person is their past.

There's an old saying, 'I would rather hear it from the horses mouth than hear it by someone else.' My family lived by that motto and we were extremely honest with each other even though it might hurt sometimes. To have a completely honest relationship, a person has to come clean with his or her future mate.

I was curious about Kyle's past, so I asked and he told me all the sordid details. He had served time, nine months, at the 'Point', the State Prison at the south end of the Salt Lake Valley. I had passed by the formidable place many a time on the way to Salt Lake City with my family to our happy family reunions. He had been caught with a briefcase full of marijuana with intent to sell. He was nineteen at the time and had been attending University of Utah as a student when this occurred. He then proceeded to tell me about his hippie days while attending college in which he organized communes that practiced 'free love' in which he participated in 'very freely'.

He then proceeded to tell me that when he was eight years old living in Panama, he intently watched three little naked street urchins sodomizing each other in public. They didn't seem to have a care or worry in the world. He went home that night and asked mightily of the Lord to take away his calling that he knew he had in the Lord and become black and not have any worries like those urchins. He fully felt the Lord would answer his prayers the next day and was disappointed that he was not black when he woke up the next morning. He did notice, however, that from then on, no one ever told him he could do better than he was doing in his life. So that made him happy. He also told me he would steal things and had been proud about how he got away with it. He also told me how he had did things to his sisters he shouldn't have done.

There were more things he told me, but I don't want to get into them. He told me that he had been married to a ballerina named Cynthia, but had no children by her.

"What made you decide to repent from all of these things and turn to the Lord?" I asked. I had never heard of anything like his story in all of my life. I didn't even know people who had ever lived anything close to what he had just told me. I was beginning to wonder why the Lord had told me to marry this man. Clearly, he had done many things in his life that were not only illegal but immoral. But, I also had done some immoral things that I was currently repenting of. I had not filled my full year up of living righteously to get my temple recommend and he had.

"I felt that it was time to get my act together and get married in the temple and raise a family," he thoughtfully replied.

Surely, he had a lot to repent of, but as I look at him as he is now, he is so straight, he almost squeaks. He's almost straighter that me.

I first had to tell him that I married Vince because I loved him, or so I thought. That marriage only lasted a year and a half before he went back to his mother.

I then told him how I fell away from the church after being burned by so many returned missionaries. I started dating non-Mormons who had only the world's morals. (There were no scruples about having sex on our first or second date.) I finally dated a Hispanic man that raped me on our first date. My self esteem went to an all time low and I continued to let him abuse me until I became pregnant.

When I told him I was pregnant and asked him if he was going to marry me, he adamantly said there was no way he was going to marry me.

I wasn't about to raise a bastard child without help from a husband. I already had one child to support without a husband, I certainly didn't need two children. I then proceeded to do everything I could do to lose the baby including overdosing on birth control pills.

After many attempts, I went to my mother for help. She stood by me and took me to an abortion clinic. Apparently, through all my attempts, including getting some kind of shot from a doctor, I had already lost the baby. I had never been so relieved. I was happy that my mother supported me and still loved me even though I had made the mistake.

After that period of time, I decided to come back to the Church and live right again.

After this discussion which left much for me to ponder and probably him, also, we went our separate ways after hugging and kissing each other. I prayed a mighty prayer that night as to why the Lord wanted me to marry him, especially after what he told me this night.

Saturday, August 2, 1975
Dear Journal,

I was somewhat apprehensive about calling my parents today when I probably shouldn't have been. I wanted then to be happy about Kyle and let them know how I was getting along. I realize I was putting too many things ahead of me, which is the way Satan wants us to do.

When I finally did call, they were all happy to hear from Ann and me. They were tickled about me getting married. Ann and I talked with all the family including Suzie and Darleen whom Ann misses so very much. Suzie, Darleen and Ann had become very close to each other while I was living in Terra Bella after my divorce from Vince. They are only a few years older than her and loved playing with her.

Today, after cooking a delicious meal of fried chicken, veges and cake, Kyle told me I will make an excellent wife because I'm a "domestic." I had never heard of that term before. Apparently that's what they called their hired maids while living in Panama. He then told me his former wife, the dancer, was far from being one, but he still loved her.

I feel we will have a happy marriage.

We went looking for houses today. We looked at three houses. We looked at a little tiny white house with one bedroom, a nice size brick house and a brown house. The tiny white house was the worst house of all. It was so dilapidated and old I really didn't see us living in it all. However, it did have a nice river running behind it and a quite a bit of land around it.

Sunday, August 3, 1975

We went over to see my sister Terri. Since I was kind of leery about visiting her after having a strange phone conversation with her, it was almost like she was scared to talk to me, I didn't know what to expect.

My qualms were settled when Kyle, Ann, and myself arrived at her home. She seemed very happy to see us. Jim was fishing with his buddies and she felt free and easy. She explained that she was glad that he went with his friends so he could get acquainted with them so she wouldn't be his only friend.

She then showed us how she trained her beautiful German shepherd dog. He did many dog tricks. She explained to us that until he would allow her to have children, that the dog would take their place.

When Jim got home, he was so upset to see that any of her family was at their home. He let it be very clear by slamming doors, cussing very loudly, and then telling her to get rid of us that he didn't want any of us around her or him. We apologized and quickly left.

It didn't take a rocket scientist to see where their marriage was. We also felt that if she ever did wake up to his controlling abuse and leave him, that he might decide to kill her.

Kyle then stated that we might be the ones directly responsible for their divorce. He then jokingly stated that he wouldn't mind her being one of his wives.

My sister, Terri, is a very beautiful woman, with lovely freckles all over her body. She was wearing a skimpy halter-top with short shorts. She also had an hour glass figure to die for. I remember taking measurements when were teens. She had a 36-23-36 figure while I barely had boyish figure with a larger waist and size 'B' bust. The only thing that I had that was a 36 was my hips. Try as I might, I never had the classic hour-glass figure. My sisters would kind of make fun of my figure. Oh well, such is life. I didn't wonder too much that my future husband made a comment like this.

After the visit to our visit to my sister, we went to sign papers for the little white house, much to my disappointment. Kyle had signed the papers for the nicer brown house and the white house earlier today, but as we were coming back from Salt Lake City, we were going to look at the brick house. But then Kyle turned off the freeway when he shouldn't have. I asked why.

"I feel that we ought to buy the white house with the one-third acre on it," he replied.

As he said it, the Holy Spirit filled my soul and I felt right about his decision.

I was rather skeptical about house buying on Sunday, for it is the Lords day. I hope the Lord will forgive us.

Monday, August 4, 1975
Dear Journal,

Today was a very busy day. We did so much running around. We painted and cottage-cheesed a ceiling in one of Kyle's brothers' houses. We did this from 10 a.m. in the morning until midnight. Ann was such a cheerful little helper. She helped me spread newspaper all over the floor and then helped me gather it up after we were finished.

After much discussion with Kyle about how much time we were spending together and how little time I was studying, we decided it would be a good idea for me to quit school. I was not too unhappy about it since we were going to get married. I was hoping to continue my education, but I could see now was not the time.

Wednesday, August 5
Dear Journal,

Today I informed my piano teacher that I was quitting my lessons. All of us then went to Salt Lake City to shop at the lumber yard/hardware store called Chris and Dicks. We picked up fencing material to put a fence around the property of the little white house. It was a very long day. I don't know how that little purple Ford Cortina station wagon fit all the fencing in it, let alone carry it. It is such a dilapidated old car that you can see the ground as you go down the road.

Thursday, August 6
Dear Journal,

Today we finally got to see the inside of the little white house. It was so dank, dark and small, it was barely livable. The kitchen was barely operable with an old time metal sink – not much of an upgrade from the lime-green apartment I was living in. The bathroom was very nasty and dirty with rotting wood on the floor and crud on the walls. The bedroom was disappointingly small with no place to put Ann. She would have to sleep in the living room. The walls were a sickening gray color that had come that way with age. The home would take a lot of work just to make it livable. Oh well, lets look on the bright side. We have strong hands and minds and we'll be able t remodel the inside when we get situated.

Kyle seemed more troubled about the boundary issues than the house. He doesn't want to put up the fence and wants the present owner to do it. We do not want to be enemies already with our future neighbors.

I am reading the <u>Screwtape Letters</u>, by C.S. Lewis. This is a book that Kyle suggested I read. It's a very good book on how the Satan operates in tempting us. I'm also reading the Book or Mormon as part of the commitment I made to myself to read all of the scriptures completely one chapter a day.

Sunday, August 17
Dear Journal,

My former Bishop Christenson sent a letter to me and my present Bishop Blackham. It explained that I had morally transgressed the law of God and suggested that Bishop Blackham should interview me before he decides whether or not to give me a temple recommend.

When I went to Bishop Blackham's office to talk with him, I was a little worried. We talked about all of my past and told him that I had truly repented of my sins and felt that I was worthy of marrying Kyle at this time.

I had expressed my concerns about my interview with Kyle and he stated, "If the Lord wants you to get married in the temple, he'll arrange for you to get your recommend."

Today was also stake conference. It was a lovely session on families in the home. We took Ann to a Junior Sunday School in the Bonneville Ward. We enjoyed ourselves and she appeared to enjoy herself. There were many children in which to play with. She was happy to see us, however when we came back to get her.

At this time you might say I am Kyle's main helper. I help him clean the church. He is a janitor at the church along with taking care of all of his family's houses in Provo. Ray, the main custodian, is on vacation and it is falling on us to do all of the janitorial work. The building is under remodeling construction, so it is a rather daunting job to clean the church.

I learned a lot about cheerios and 'cousins' of cheerios all through the church. This is a very popular staple to entertain and placate the future missionaries of the church. The little edibles are indeed difficult to clean. Of course, Ann is always by my side.

By the time we were finished with everything, all of us were exhausted.

I received a letter from Mom and Dad about their concerns about Kyle and I blowing our chances of going to the temple, especially considering my past history. I wrote back assuring them that our pasts only made us more determined to make it to the temple with pure hearts and clean hands.

That's one thing I appreciated about Kyle, He was a gentleman and does not put his hands where he shouldn't. In fact I was beginning to wonder whether he knew how to make out at all. He has been very good about helping me to wait for sex until we are married in the temple. Neither of us wants to blow our chances of getting married in the temple. This is so different from my previous courtship with Vince.

Tuesday, we went to go see Kyle's grandmother the rest home. We were not able to make on Sunday. She was happy to see us. Her and Ann get along so well together. She reads to Ann and tells her how pretty she is. She plays little games with her. Ann simply adores visiting her.

Chapter 9

New Beginnings

September 6, 1975
Dear Journal,
So many events have passed since I last wrote to you and I decided I had better not delay writing any longer. I will have to go back and recap what has happened.

August 21.
My parents came from California for my Mom's 35th year Granite High School reunion. They phoned us to see where we were and arranged things so we could them. We showed them our house and property. They like the property with the lovely trees and river running behind the house, but they were not impressed with little white house. Of course, I didn't much blame them.

"It needs a lot of work and it is very small. Too small for a family," my mother bluntly stated. Of course, my mother always stated the truth bluntly.

My father mentioned that he would help to paint the place and offered a little money to help us out. This was very much appreciated.

August 23,
Kyle and I went to Dr. Croft to get our blood test results and doctor examinations to get our marriage license. We also worked at the church cleaning it for six straight hours and then went to Salt Lake City to visit my parents at my Grandma's house. We had let Ann go with them, thank goodness.

They were glad to see us and stated they liked Kyle. Kyle liked them, also. He made the comment, "I've talked more with you in one night than in the two and a half years of being married to my first wife, Cynthia's parents."

Of course, this was another tidbit of information that I did not know before.

We then had to go back to Provo to lock up the church about midnight.

Sunday, August 24th

I had my recommend signed by the Stake president. I also led the singing at church today. Kyle had informed me not to long in the recent past that he wanted to get married on the 26th of August instead of the first of September. He told the Bishop this. The Bishop didn't think there was anything wrong with the idea.

I was fairly skeptical because for one thing, we didn't have any place to live. We also had no wedding ring, no wedding dress, no beds, no furniture . . . nothing.

"Faith . . . . faith . . . . faith," I kept on reminding myself. "The Lord will prepare me/us if it's his will that this wedding is to be accomplished."

When the time came to get married two days later, the things of the world didn't seem to matter to me any longer. This seemed to the banner theme of our future.

After we went to see the bishop, we then had to see Stake President Cracroft. It was an interesting meeting. The first comment he made upon meeting me was, "I would like to meet this person who thinks she can live with Kyle for eternity and who has already spent some time with him."

The statement was a rather peculiar one in that I think the President already figured that it would take a special type of person to marry Kyle even before he met me. He then brought Kyle and me together for a very important lecture that we could use for the rest of our lives.

The main points were:

Not to judge or put ourselves above others. He stated that both Kyle and I knew the gospel more than most people that he has met. He then stated that we really didn't need to go to church, but go anyway, because the people at the church needed our love.

Not to become too elitist (the perfect Mormon type) so as to not go overboard and eventually fall away from the Church or be too liberal. Either extreme is not healthy.

Not to have self righteousness, but have humbleness.

Make sure Kyle and I use the priesthood in our home for times we are sick and blessings from husband to wife and father to children.

Don't have the problem of generalizing the Church to everybody and advancing too rapidly in our knowledge and understanding so we don't leave others behind.

To be one in Christ Jesus when we go to church and take the sacrament at sacrament meeting.

When we got ready to leave, he said an astounding statement. He said, "The Lord has brought you two together through thick and thin to be together."

He then looked at me and stated, "You know more about the hidden mysteries of God than anyone he had ever met."

Then he told both of us that we were both descended from Royal blood. I knew this to be true for my side because of the Presidents, kings and queens that had been traced through my Grandma Nelson's diligent genealogy work she had devoted her life to. This probably held true for his side, also. I just hadn't seen his genealogy yet.

Monday, August 25th,

Everything has gotten so crazy; it almost seems there is no time to breathe. My parents came over to see us. They took Ann with them to Salt Lake City so we could have a little time to prepare for the wedding. Kyle was making our wedding rings out of silver wire and solder. They were going to be puzzle rings like the ones they use in the Middle East according to Kyle. I had never heard of such a thing let alone about the Middle East.

Just before he went to solder mine, he dropped it. Like Humpty Dumpty, he couldn't put it back together. So, I wouldn't have a ring. He did manage to solder a wire ring for me and one for himself so we could at least have something to use in the ceremony.

By this time, it was 4:30 A.M.

Tuesday, August 26th,

We then had to go move my stuff out of his brother's house #1111, so some people could move in. We just piled all of our stuff next to my car in the garage. Kyle then took a shower. He desperately needed one. Then we took turns driving to Manti because it was an hour and one-half drive. We were both so tired, we had to have a little nap while the other was driving on the way to Manti. We had to be there by 7 A.M. We arrived at 6:15 A.M. I tried to catch a few winks in the back of the old purple Ford Cortina stationwagon, but sleep had fled my eyes.

We had zero sleep for 24 hours before we were married.

Going through the temple was so beautiful and so spiritual, that I didn't even think of sleep the whole time. My mother went through with me. Among the party that went through with us were two sets of Uncles and Aunts on his side. My Mom and Dad and Grandma went through on my side. This turn-out of relatives was pretty impressive in a family for such a short notice. His Uncles and Aunts seemed to be very nice people. They lived near the Manti Temple and did a lot of work in that Temple.

It is one of the choicest experiences I have ever had. I want to go through the temple as often as I can in my life. I don't ever want to do anything to jeopardize the opportunity.

After we were married, we went to Richgrove to check out a motel room. While there, I discovered what kind of husband he would be in our marriage. Much to my chagrin, he was not much of a lover. Maybe it was too bad that I had such an excellent lover in my first husband so I would be able to compare the two. I didn't want to tell him that he didn't let me climax. Maybe he didn't have a clue what a woman's climax was. I was willing to let this important fact go because we had just been married in the sacred temple and my husband is now the head of the house. If this was how he made love, so be it. This brand of slam-bam-thank you, Ma'am sex (not love making) was doomed to be often and never improved.

We were both so exhausted that we slept and slept until dark. We then got up and bought a shrimp basket at a local drive-in. Then Kyle got a box of ice cream cones and I bought some fruit. His brilliant idea was we could eat the fruit in the cones. He was later sorry he bought the cones, in that we soon ran out of money.

We also bought two pairs of garments apiece which was a relief for him. He had had to borrow a pair from a friend that was too small and they were seriously cutting into his crotch.

Wednesday, August 27th,

We drove back to Provo and went to sleep again. We then went to Salt Lake City to a "small" reception that my parents put on for us in my Grandma's back yard. Thirty people, all relatives, showed up. We had hamburgers and cake – it was a lot of fun. I was very grateful to my parents for doing this for us on such very short notice. We also celebrated Kyle's birthday with candles on the wedding cake. When they were lit, they almost burned the little design in the cake.

We left Ann again with my parents. She didn't appreciate the fact. But Kyle and I felt she would have a good time for a few more days with her grandparents for a few more days until Kyle and I could get a place for us to live in.

Thursday, August 28th,

We moved a man named Roger out of our little white house that we had bought. I never imagined that one person could make such a mess. We then spent Wednesday night in Kyle's old basement apartment because the little white house was unlivable in the shape it was in. It was going to take a massive amount of work just to shovel the junk out of the tiny home.

Randy, my old dancing partner in Porterville, and his wife Terrill, came by the apartment. They did not appear to be too happy with each other. Is this the doomed life that most married young Mormon people seem to have? I thought to myself. I do hope their marriage works out.

I remember when someone had mentioned to him and me that maybe we could get married. After all we had known each other ever since we were babies and were good friends all of our lives, he had retorted, "It would be like marrying my sister if we got married!"

I mentioned this to Kyle later, and we both had a little chuckle about it.

Friday, August 29th,

Kyle and I worked exhaustingly to clean the little white house and finally got it partially cleaned. I didn't know someone could be such a slob. Fortunately, it was small so we got most of it cleaned.

The next day we cleaned the church. With all this cleaning we were doing I was beginning to wonder if we could ever see the end.

We then went to Salt Lake City to pick up Ann because my parents were leaving to go back to California. I was sad to see them go back home. They were such a help in watching Ann when I needed them at this very busy, trying time in my life.

We said our goodbyes and hugs and kisses. And then we headed back to our little white house in Provo.

Sunday, August 31st,

I led the singing again. It was such a spiritual uplift and a pleasant change from all the cleaning and madness from the previous week. Ann seemed to be happy to be with me and her new daddy. She liked playing with the children in Sunday school.

Monday, September 1st,

We stopped and fixed a couple's car on the side of the road. Kyle has some knowledge of mechanics and doesn't mind helping others. The couple's names were Jerry and Laura.

We then went over to a woman's house by the name of Victoria. She had invited Kyle, myself and Ann over to have dinner with her. This woman was the person Kyle had been living with before he decided to get married in the temple. Apparently, that was not her desire, also, so their relationship deteriorated.

"So," I asked, wondering a little, "why are we having dinner with this woman?'

"I don't see what's wrong with you being friends with my ex-girlfriends," he answered, as though this were to be the norm for the rest of the marriage. Apparently I was to be friends with all of his ex-lovers from here on.

Then Jerry and Laura, who needed a place to live, were invited by Kyle to stay in our backyard. This looked like the beginning of a long relationship with this couple. Everything we had we shared with them. That day, all I had was a salad to split with them and my family. The next day, they treated us to a pizza. It was very good.

Jerry started cleaning the yard and I started to do my long overdue laundry by hand.

Then came a Judy T. I found out later that she was also after Kyle to marry him. She was Mormon, brunette and had a daughter named Emily, which eight years old. Her and Ann got along wonderfully. I asked Kyle why he didn't marry her. He answered, "Her daughter was too old."

At the time, I couldn't understand what the age of the daughters was made any difference in getting married. I would later figure this puzzle out.

Saturday, we worked in the church. Ray was back from his vacation. It was amazing how much difference it made to have him back! Work went so much faster.

It's so wonderful being married to Kyle. I love it when he calls to me, "Come here, Carla, if you have a minute. I want to talk to you." Then what he has to say is, "I love you." It thrills me to pieces to have someone love me.

Chapter 10

'Louder Than'

Sunday, September 21, 1975
Dear Journal,

So many things have happened during the past two weeks that I have had a hard time writing to you. I apologize. It appalls me to see how fast everything is whizzing by. I even tried to space things out for three weeks instead the two I had.

Today was such a beautiful Sunday. I enjoyed serving the Lord by leading the Junior Sunday School songs. I feel the spirits of the little children while they sing. I have people come up to me and tell me what a wonderful job I do, but I give all the credit to the Lord.

Today was ward conference and the message was for the wives to encourage their husbands to do their home teaching. They also encouraged the wives to help their husbands to magnify their priesthood. They also mentioned that spending time with your children is more important than any worldly gifts.

It reminded me about the lack thereof in the entire melee that I have been going through ever since I married Kyle. I barely have enough time to breathe, let alone spend with my daughter.

Kyle and I sang in the choir a song by the title, "Still, Still with Thee." It was such a peaceful and beautiful song that chills went up and down my back while singing it.

Did I mention about getting to serve as Junior Sunday School for such a short time? I'll bet you're wondering why. Couldn't guess? We are moving! Aw . . . want the details now? Well, you'll just have to wait because I have a lot of catching up to do.

Sunday, September 7th,

Judy T's VW van broke down around five. We pushed her into the shop. We had to pick up Kyle's Grandma at 6:30 p.m. We then invited Jerry and Laura along with Kyle's grandmother and other friends to Family Home Evening. We had seven people crowded into the little white house. Both Kyle and I finally got to turn in at 12:30 a.m.

Tuesday, September 9th,

After three and one-half hour sleep, Kyle and I woke up to attend the opening day of the new Provo Temple. We were having a lot of bad feelings between us, perhaps because of lack of sleep and privacy in our marriage. This dissipated in the temple because the spirit there was so wonderful. When we exited the temple, we began fighting again. It was a recurring subject of his that would prevail through our marriage I found out. He accused me of not having my thoughts organized and I couldn't think right. Therefore, I couldn't talk right.

I was getting fed up about him continually mentioning this fault of mine to me. I thought that I was just fine and I let him know I didn't appreciate him criticizing me continually. Of course, he could always out yell me. Once again, he left me in tears.

We went to get Judy T. so she could get her van out of the shop. Kyle said something quite rude about her roommate, Bonnie, which really upset Judy. She demanded to be taken home. Apparently, she couldn't handle Kyle's choice of words either.

When we got home, Kyle and I settled our disagreement. We tried to not let a day go by without settling our differences. Then exhausted after the day's events, we took a nap.

When Kyle woke up, he decided he was going to join the National Guard to get his prison record erased and go back to college to get his pre-law degree. He had me read his mothers' letter concerning this matter.

Wednesday, September 10th,

Kyle went to Salt Lake City to see whether he could get into the University of Utah. He figured that since he had already started there, he would lose credits transferring to BYU. He would also have to take four years of religion in two years. The 'U' accepted him in fifteen seconds.

Thursday, September 11th,

Since Kyle was going to the 'U', we decided that we would need an apartment in Salt Lake City so he wouldn't have to commute. We went up with his old girlfriend, Victoria, to look. We then went around looking on our own after we had dropped her off at her friends' house. We came across an old mansion that was used during the polygamists' time as a polygamists' house. Kyle explained that he wouldn't mind fixing it. His old hippie buddy that happened to live there suggested Kyle could buy it if he put in an offer. The lady that owned it would figure that Kyle would renovate the home.

Kyle called the owners up and offered $20,000 for the home. It was getting late, so we decided to go to my Grandma's home and crash. She was happy to see our little family.

The old mansion was a wreck – the whole bottom floor was a mess with people living in squalor wherever they could lay a sleeping bag. The walls were in bad need of repair. I could see the brick and lathe and plaster beneath what was left of the wall paper. The kitchens and bathrooms were a disaster with leaking pipes. I couldn't see us ever being able to repair it. The upstairs was somewhat promising with two apartments in them. I would take the top one facing south with a nice balcony and a decent bathroom and two bedrooms. It took many man hours to clean that apartment. We rented the back apartment to Jerry and Laura.

Sunday, September 14th,

I led the singing for probably the last time in our present ward. I thoroughly enjoy church. We then went to sign our papers with earnest money for the mansion. We visited some old friends of Kyle's named Rocky and some other of his old friends. I was fast finding that Salt Lake City was his old stomping grounds when he was a full-blown hippy. There were many hippie friends and former commune girlfriends there. He was certainly in his glory. I would have never dreamed there was such a subculture such as this in this glorious city.

We then attended our future ward in the Avenues. We seemed to be accepted well by the people there. We then trekked back to Provo in the purple Cortina stationwagon.

Monday, September 15th,

We had a busy day showing people our little white house on the river. We actually had a quiet home evening all to ourselves. Jerry and Laura, still living in the tent on the property next to river in their tent were a little bummed out about having to move from their habitat, and didn't feel like attending.

Tuesday, the 16th

We were planning to go to the temple this morning, but somehow slept through our alarm. I ended up showing the house to several other people. One man came by twice and told us he was going home to get his "boss" (wife) and let her come and look at it.

Wednesday, the 17th,

Ann was sick all day, so I was concerned about going to Salt Lake City that evening to look at the mansion to see what we could fix so we could live in it. We had talked about renovating the garage. We then climbed into the attic and saw how big that was and considered renovating that. I just didn't see where we were going to get the money for all of these projects. We barely had enough to pay our bills and food.

By the time we finally go a thermometer into Ann's mouth, she had 104.8 temp. I was getting very concerned about her condition. We then went to Francie's house, another ex-girlfriend of Kyle's and called a doctor. He advised us to bathe her in tepid water and give her half an aspirin in orange juice. This was immediately followed.

I then asked Kyle to give her a priesthood blessing, in which he promptly refused. His excuse was, "When she is old enough to ask, he might give her one."

I was somewhat dismayed, but dared not make any mention of this fact because since my husband is the head of the household, I must honor his decision.

Fortunately, Ann was much better the next morning.

Thursday, the 18th,

We were concerned about getting a loan for buying and renovating the old mansion. We needed to sell our little house on the river to fund some of the renovation. I found that Kyle apparently has a lot of very rich friends. One of them is named Rick. He owned a camera shop in Salt Lake City and always had about twenty hippie looking friends renovating the shop. Kyle also informed me that this young man took a mountain climbing expedition to Mt. Everest. He didn't make it all the way to the top, but made it most of the way up. You do have to have plenty of money to do that.

Kyle informed me that Rick had said he would loan him the money if we were in a tight pinch. I wasn't used to the kind of money that Kyle's friends had.

The stress of everything in the air continually was putting a strain on our marriage already. We stayed at my Grandma's again. We seemed to get part of problems solved, but were too exhausted to do much else.

Friday, the 19th,

After doing our regular work for the day, Kyle and I talked until 2:30 a.m. settling our differences. I felt pretty good about this discussion and hoped it would help our marriage twenty years or more down the road. We decided we were madly in love with each other and may even like each other. We found we had many differences between us, but we would need to tolerate and communicate them. The one thing that was different in this marriage from the last was I didn't have a mother-in-law to contend with.

Indeed, I hadn't even met this one. She was still in Panama.

Saturday, the 20th,

Kyle went to work at the church alone because Ray figured there wasn't enough to keep both of busy. It was a nice change for I was once again exhausted from having only having one hour of sleep. Ann kept herself busy around the house. When Kyle came home, he patiently taught her the O's, X's and I's in the alphabet. He seems to be very patient with her.

Chapter 11

"Twinkled"

M onday, October 13, 1975
Dear Journal,
   I feel somewhat inspired to write to you today. I will earnestly continue to do so when I am inspired.

   Today was so wonderful! I had the opportunity to attend the Salt Lake Temple. I felt so spiritual and peaceful while going through the session. I had to go alone because Kyle got a job at Blue Cross, Blue Shield as a janitor for 32 hours a week and also attends school full time. We haven't been seeing very much of each other lately.

   My Grandma was kind enough to watch Ann outside the temple on the grounds. They had a fabulous time visiting all the exhibits on the grounds.

   The only thing that bothered me during the session was that I had the awful feeling of having to share sex with Kyle and all his old hippie girl-friends. I had to work hard to dispel the evil thoughts. It disturbed me so much, that I approached Kyle about it.

   "What's wrong with polygamy?" he blithely answered as if there was nothing in the world wrong with it.

   "I suppose it is a lot like your days of communal living in your hippie era," I curtly replied. "I feel that I'm sharing you with all your old commune women. The mansion that we are buying still has a commune in it! Polygamy is wrong in any form according to the Church, even though our ancestors practiced it."

   "Well, I know the laws of God," he retorted, "and according to the scriptures and Joseph Smith, there is nothing wrong with the practice."

   "Look," I argued, "One of the things that we committed in our marriage and interviews for our temple recommends was that we would stay away from any faction that believed in polygamy or we would be excommunicated. Is this what you want? I hope you are not toying with idea."

He paused, and then reassured me, "I'm not going to. Besides, you are the one I love. One thing I know for sure is this, I know that I am perfect and I'm going to be twinkled. Are you?"

I wasn't so sure I perfect enough at this time to be 'twinkled'. Being raised a Mormon, I was very familiar with the term 'twinkled'. We describe the term as being caught up and changed from mortality to immortality in a twinkling of an eye. According to the New Testament, Jesus asked his disciples what they wanted to do before he left to his father. Two of them, James and John, asked to be able stay alive and preach the gospel until he came again the second time. Jesus granted them their wish by 'twinkling' them. There were also three more that he 'twinkled' in America, according to the Book of Mormon, when they made the same request the James and John did. I made the tort reply to him, "Well, you'll just have to be twinkled without me, then."

I am getting very upset with what is going on in the mansion. After I painted, cleaned, scrubbed and put a nice hemp rug down in the kitchen and was getting somewhat used to sharing the huge house with about twenty other hippies, Kyle rented our apartment out to his old flame Francie without even letting me know about it. Apparently, she needed a place to stay before she had her baby. I am not used to women having their baby without a father. She picked the man she wanted to be her kid to look like and had sex with him to get pregnant.

She had tried to get pregnant by her dope smoking druggie friend, but his drugging made his sperm count so low that he couldn't impregnate her. So she turned to another available dick that had a good job, but was extremely abusive and she had to leave her home. So now Kyle magnanimously gives her our little apartment.

This is on top of finding out I was going to have a baby son by a voice, and a little girl to care for. I told Kyle about this revelation, but it looks like his old hippie lovers take precedence to his own wife and growing family.

Tuesday, October 14,

Today, much to my shame, my sister Terri came and paid me a visit. She was shocked to see the deplorable conditions that I was living in. She couldn't believe all the people that were literally crammed into the bottom half of the house in their slothful conditions. I found out later that she even called the Child's Welfare Services on me. I realized what condition I was in. I wasn't stupid.

"Carla," she exclaimed, "the conditions here are deplorable and Ann and yourself should not be subjected to this mess. This is not a good place to raise a little girl."

"Terri," I tearfully replied, "I'm doing the best I can under the circumstances that I am in."

I was almost glad to see her go and didn't dare tell her that I was going to be kicked out of my apartment in my house for one of Kyle's old hippie girlfriends, and would be living in the bedroom across the hall with no kitchen, bathroom or any running water whatsoever. Ann had started peeing her pants, which was odd. I already had her potty trained. It was bad enough for me to be deprived, but to deprive my only child, was unbearable to me. As for Ann's problem, I chalked it up to the stressful conditions that were happening ever since I had married Kyle.

We sold our house in Provo to the couple that the man stated we would need to get his "boss." Our payments for the mansion were $240 a month and we were making $300 a month rent from it. We started putting a roof on the dilapidated garage and putting insulation in it. Kyle came up with the bright idea to make it a "reading room" for all of his buddies.

It was such a waste of money . . . our money in which we had so little of . . . and Ann and I were being so deprived of.

I was feeling so despondent about the conditions we were in, I had nothing else to do besides watch Ann, I wrote a letter to my parents and also to my Grandmother Eggman, also called "Mom-Judy."

Besides not telling my mother and father about Ann and my deplorable condition we were in, I had heard that my great-Uncle Clyde had to have his legs cut off above his knees because of his failure to quit smoking while he had diabetes. He would not follow the doctors' orders to quit and lost his circulation.

I remember when I was a little girl, I would be visiting my "Mom-Judy" and he would come in from work after staying at Herb's Bar for a few beers. He would bring his beer in, sit down in the recliner and smoke and drink until he passed out. My grandma's house would smell like Herb's Bar. The reason I knew how Herb's Bar smelled was I had a few occasions where I had to go into the bar the fetch him.

As you probably guessed, my Dad's side of the family were not Mormons. Dad was able to convert three of his brothers to Mormonism. One was killed while working for my dad hauling potatoes right after he got out the service. My day had him work and not go home and even say "Hi" to his mother. He was so tired, and didn't drink any coffee to keep him awake, because Mormons don't drink coffee, and was killed while crossing the tracks because he fell asleep at the wheel.

Believe me, I was told this story every time I visited "Mom-Judy" until I wanted to throw up every time I heard the story.

This was my Grandma's only sibling and he was dying. I was sorry to hear about it. I let her know I loved her and gave her my condolences.

My parents wanted to know if the could sell the trailer they sold me. I had refurbished the whole trailer by putting in new carpet, new drapes, and reconditioned the wood. I also completely painted the top with aluminum coating and painted the whole trailer cream with chocolate color trim. It was really cute. I told them it was okay to sell it and keep the money. They got $2000 for it. They used the money to purchase 26 acres of oranges at a location further down the Old Stage Road and to pay for back taxes.

I wished them well and dared not ask for any money even though they would have sent me some. I didn't want them to know about what Ann and I were going through.

Sunday, October 19th,

Today, while I was sitting in church, I was inspired to write a poem. It is as follows;
Church is
    My little girl saying, "There is Jesus!"
Church is
    Seeing a loving father teach
    His retarded daughter how to read.
Church is
    Listening to the speaker and
    Really hearing what they have to say.
Church is
    Hearing the unprofessional choir
    Singing from their hearts.
Church is
    For people.
Yes, you and I.
It's sometimes said to be a
    Hospital for sinners,
But, whatever or whomever we are,
It's the spirit that matters,
And the strength which we receive in numbers,
In keeping the Lord's Commandments
On this Holy Sabbath Day.

Sometimes I feel like Abraham's wife, Sarah, when the Lord talks to me. I still can't believe he chooses to talk to me. However I know it is true beyond a shadow of a doubt. I am tired, I think I will quit for tonight. Hope to see you again, soon.

Chapter 12

Skinny Dipping

Friday, November 7th, 1975
Dear Journal,

I realize it has been a long time since I wrote to you. My lack of writing to you is getting worse instead of better. I will have to improve.

I have to watch my rose-colored glasses carefully. Kyle has changed his hours from thirty-two hours to forty hours so we can have more benefits with the birth of our first baby. He is still attending the 'U' full-time, also. He does most of his studying at work. He is getting good grades.

Sometimes, Ann and I go to work with him just to be able to see him and spend some time with him. We set up a little bed for her to sleep on and sometimes Kyle and I would catch a little nap after his work.

One night, while we were talking until 2;30 in the morning, his boss, Kay, appeared and checked up on Kyle and his work. She didn't say much about me being there, and it was a good thing he was awake at the time. She was very particular about the janitorial job and wanted things to be just right. I also became friends with one Kyle's old friend who worked in the boiler room. His name was Joe.

I've been very busy making Ann doll clothes for her little doll for Christmas. I never seem to have enough money for extras, let alone food. I'm also making Ann some clothes. The Lord knows she needs some. I haven't been able to buy her much of anything for her needs.

I took Ann to the doctor about her urination problem. The doctor found she had a bladder infection and advised me to not let her have any bubble baths. Soap in the water causes the water to become more able to travel up little girl's urinary track and causes the infections. I will also need to use cotton panties instead of silk-like ones, because the latter also causes infections. I don't know how she will like not taking bubble baths, because this was one of her favorite activities. I will get her more toys to play with while she is in the bathtub.

We are working on putting a floor in the attic. We have run out of money when we could have put a bathroom in the room we will be moving into in this dreadful mansion. Kyle wouldn't work with my suggestion, so here we are with nothing but nice flooring in a huge attic that we can do nothing with.

Francie is due to move into our apartment by December, just in time for her to have her baby. I don't know how we are going to do everything we need to do and survive when she moves in to our apartment.

Kyle and I were invited to a birthday party at his friend Rick's house for his friend Rick. Wow! Now I know why Kyle said he could get money from his friend! The opulence of the house was unreal. I didn't know that there were such nice homes in Salt Lake City. They had all kinds of catered food with all the booze anyone would want. They also had a hot-air balloon that I rode in for a few minutes before the storm coming in grounded it.

I also did something I thought I would never do, I skinny-dipped! This was in their very large indoor heated pool. Everyone else was skinny dipping and encouraged me to do the same. I had never skinny dipped in my life, especially in the presence of other people. The only time I ever got close to someone skinny dipping was up in California Hot Springs when I was dating a very handsome young jack-Mormon man that I met at church was hiking the mountains. Some people had dammed the springs and were skinny dipping in the hot water. He spied them before I did and said, "Don't look!"

"Don't look at what?" I very innocently asked. Believe me, this was before I was married the first time and had not had any water under the bridge, and had never seen a naked man before. Curiosity got the better of me, and I peeked over the cliff. There they were, in all their glory. My face turned all shades of beet red. I quickly stated, "Let's get out of here." I practically ran all the way back to his car. Vince and this young man almost had an altercation one time about which house I was going to; his or Vince's. This was after a dance recital in Visalia the young man went to so he could see me. Vince came late and they fought over who was going to get my luggage. Vince won.

Now here I was, seriously contemplating joining them at this delicious swimming pool. Of course, I waited until most of the skinny dippers were gone, then I stripped my clothes off, very discreetly, and carefully entered the warm, glorious water. What a thrill! I kept to myself and hoped that not many people noticed me. I got out after a while.

Chapter 13

South Jordan

July 9, 1976

Dear Journal,

I realize it has been such a long time that I have written to you. So much has happened since I last wrote.

The mansion in the Avenues was becoming so cumbersome to us, and believe me, I really complained when I got stationed in just one bedroom in my own house with my daughter, while Francie got my apartment. The bedroom was like a one-cell prison, only worse. I didn't even have a head or running water of any kind. It was very demeaning to have to ask Francie if I could use her bathroom. When she was gone, I had to use Jerry and Laura's bathroom. Needless to say, Ann's and my hygiene were pathetic. I know an inmate would not go through what we were going through. We had to beg for our baths. I never had to do this in my entire life. Even when there were no baths when we were kids in the apple orchard, at least we had an outhouse and a faucet to wash our dirty bodies with.

I was so thrilled when we finally sold the place in March to a prude of a lady and bought a house in South Jordan. The address is 11380 South 2200 West. It's way down in the south valley. The house had a nice yard, it had a large kitchen, three bedrooms that needed work, it ran on coal for heat in the winter, and had about one-half acre of land with it. I was so thrilled, I planted peaches and apples and apricots and a huge garden. I canned so many beets that summer I can't remember how many I canned. We even have cats.

We have a cat that would catch a mouse and bounce the mouse off of the ceiling. It would fall to the floor with a bounce and the cat would bounce it back to the ceiling. It was so fun to watch. Ann and I would watch the cat for as long as it would take to bounce that mouse before she would eat it.

We have another cat that loved to corner flies and eat them. We lived right next to a horse training coral, so we had plenty of flies to go around. We would open the door to let a few flies in and love to sit and watch that cat eat the flies. This was definitely heaven.

Kyle and I tore down the bowing sheets of particle board in the bedrooms and installed sheetrock. We mudded and painted them and made beautiful bedrooms. We got a washing machine box and painted it for a playhouse for Ann. She loved it and spent many an hour playing in the box.

In the third bedroom, we put shelves in so Kyle could have an office to do his studies.

It is so wonderful to have a home of our own and away from the city! We were away from the slum of hippiedom in that old mansion. I am so happy!

I'm almost ready to have our little boy. We've already named him George Washington L. Kyle wanted to me to deliver him around the 4th of July since this was our great nation's Bicentennial. The doctor said he will be born around the fifteenth. Kyle has threatened to give Castor oil if I didn't hurry up and deliver the baby. It's pretty awesome to be giving birth to a baby boy named George Washington around this time. Just think, this only happens once in a lifetime.

Right now, we are so in debt that Kyle has talked about selling our little house and living in a tent. After all I have gone through this past year since being married to Kyle, the idea makes me shudder. I keep assuring him we will be okay. The Lord will bless us somehow if we have faith in him. He talks about building a dome house. "That sounds great, but how are we going build one while we are under so much debt?" I asked him.

We are also looking for a pickup so we can carry around our furniture and belongings if we needed to move again. We'll also have a camper shell on the back of it so we can have a place to sleep.

I received a summons from Vince after letting him have Ann for a month and a half. Kyle has asked me to put in detail to the best of my knowledge what happened from April 20 to June 8th with Vince and Ann.

As I recall, we went to California to a Science Fiction/Trekie convention in Los Angeles. Kyle and his buddies had published Science Fiction magazines and other memorabilia of Clingons, Starship Enterprise, etc. for the convention.

It was the most amazing convention filled with all kinds of people dressed in almost nothing, men and women, looking a lot like the Star Trek show I loved to watch in the '60's. There was everything imaginable there, from holographs, to advanced computer sciences. I had never seen anything like this in my life and quite impressed with the massive display that was at the convention. This was their religion and they were very fanatical about it. Of course, so were Kyle and his buddies fanatical about what they were doing.

We then went to visit Kyle's sister. This would be the second member of his family I would meet. She was an extremely beautiful blond, with big breasts and trim figure. Of course, she made my breasts feel small, but I was used to that by now. I was also very pregnant, so shape didn't really matter at this time. She also had a very nice husband and he was cordial to us. We stayed with them a couple of days and then went to see my Mom and Dad in Terra Bella.

While we were visiting my parents, "Mom-Judy" called us on the phone to inform us that Mike H., Vince's father had died. No one had told us this before. I called for Vince at his mothers old number and talked to his mother gave her our condolences. She let me know that Vince was married and gave me his address and phone number.

I then called Vince and gave him my condolences. He then asked me how Ann was. He hadn't seen Ann in a year and wanted to see her. I talked it over with Kyle who didn't see any reason why Ann couldn't stay with her Dad for the month that he requested.

The woman Vince had married was a Physician's Assistant and had her own office. He had met her by taking some of his help into her for injuries they had while working on his farm. Vince and her were married in the Catholic church and were living across the street from the Catholic church in what was the Nun's house in Dinuba. She sounded like a very good woman and I was sincerely happy for him. She had two adopted children from a previous marriage and they appeared to be very happy when Kyle and I went over to visit them.

Ann was not too happy about staying there and us leaving her there with them, but we felt it was the right thing to do at the time.

Kyle and I then went back to LA to the convention then back to South Jordan. I missed Ann so much, that when someone asked where she was on Mother's Day at church, I broke down crying.

A month later, when we were due to pick up Ann up, Vince asked for another month. I didn't want to let him have her for another month, but after much tormented prayer, I felt I should write him a letter saying that I objected, but it was his decision to keep her. Of course, he decided to do so.

We had an agreement with Vince, that he would let us talk to her every Monday night. Vince and Sheila were at first reluctant to do this because Ann would cry every time we talked to her and wanted to come home. But, Kyle stuck to his guns and held them to the plan.

One Monday night, we called first to Vince and Sheila's home, then to his mother's home. She told us that Vince and his family were at the coast. When they finally arrived back home on Wednesday, we phoned. Ann was with Vince in Dinuba for a graduation for one of her half-sister's graduation.

When we were finally able to get hold of Sheila, Kyle told them how he felt about not being notified of the Ann's whereabouts according to their agreement with us. She indicated that we would be informed in advance if there was any change in the plans for Monday nights.

The very next Monday evening, June 7th, once again there was no one home at Vince's house, and this time, not even his mother was home. We were so concerned that something had happened that we called the fire station, police station, hospital, his brother, and even his lawyer. We finally were able to get hold of Vince at midnight our time. When asked what was going on by Kyle, Vince didn't have very much to say at first. After much arguing back and forth, Kyle asked, "How good is your word, Vince?"

Vince answered, "As good as golden." He then proceeded to tell us that he wanted us to sign a paper stating that he wanted Ann every three months until she was in first grade stating that Kindergarten was not important. After arguing with Kyle on this issue, he threatened to hang up.

This revelation about how Vince was upset Kyle and I so much, we didn't know what to do. It looked as if Vince was holding Ann hostage and we didn't know what to do. We prayed and the answer came to us to call my former Bishop Christenson and Lawyer.

We poured our hearts out to him on the midnight hour. He patiently listened, and then recommended that we go pick her up immediately. We asked him if we should get a restraining order, and he said no. Just go pick her up. We trusted his word and left for California an hour later at 2 a.m. in the morning in our purple Ford Cortina.

There was some consternation about this trip because I was now eight months pregnant and didn't know how I would travel, but I figured my pioneer ancestors crossed the plains in many conditions, I could at least go to California in the beat-up purple Cortina and pick up my daughter.

We arrive in Dinuba, California, at 5 p.m. the next day after driving non-stop, except for potty stops and fill-ups on gas and eating occasionally. We first went to Vince's house across from the Catholic church and no one was home. We then went to his mother's house. As we were heading there, I was becoming quite apprehensive that things might go wrong. I feared we might have an all out fight with Vince, so we stopped and had a prayer. When we arrived at Vince's mothers' house, we found Ann playing out in the front yard. Kyle went to tell Vince's mother that we were taking Ann.

"You're crazy!" she stated. She was very surprised to see us. "You shouldn't take her like this!"

We said our quick goodbye, and left with the Ann with what she had on. We stopped in Fresno to get her some other clothes and some shoes. We then continue to go through Fresno and north on Highway 41 through the

Tioga pass and through the middle of Nevada on a little highway I never knew existed.

It was so wonderful to have my daughter back. Ann was very talkative and told us all about her stay with her Daddy. We camped out for two nights on the way back home. It was surprisingly cold in Nevada.

When we arrived at our house, we called Vince and Sheila that everything was fine and we were home.

Chapter 14

Bicentennial Baby

September 18, 1976
Dear Journal,

It's been a long time since I wrote in you. As you probably already guessed, George Washington L. was born. Yes it was boy, just like the voice said it would be.

He was born July 22, 1976 at 4:06 a.m. He was seven pounds and 21 inches long. He was jaundiced because his liver didn't adjust fast enough and had to be put under lights. He was covered with a fine white fur all over his body. He reminded me of Esau the twin of Jacob. He was such a beautiful baby and smiled a big smile when he saw me. The nurse excused the smile as gas because she had never seen a newborn baby smile like he did, but I knew it wasn't.

Because of the distance of the hospital to our home in South Jordan, about 40 mile, and lack of reliable transportation, we arranged it with Blue Cross to let me stay at the hospital for the length of time it took for George to get well of his jaundice. I was also nursing him for I am a firm believer that nursing is the best thing for the baby's health. When the nurses went to put the cotton balls on George's eyes to shield them from the infra-red lights, they later told me they had never seen a baby fight them the way he did. The nurses nick-named him, "Gorgeous George," after the famous wrestler, and they also told me that he would make a good Olympic boxer.

Kyle stayed by my side the whole time while reading the book of Lee Harvey Oswald, President Kennedy's alleged assassin.

"It would be nice to have more children," he expressed one time to my surprise.

"Aren't you the one that was in the Zero Population Club?" I jokingly replied.

"Yes, I was at one time," he thoughtfully replied, "but this has changed a lot of my feelings about things."

After taking a long look at this man and thinking how different this situation was from my first husband; indeed, I used to beg him to have another baby in which he flatly refused and made sure I couldn't, I answered, "We need to wait a little while before having another child. It's not good for a woman to have babies too close together. When I get back on my feet and after George is weaned in about a year, then we can consider having another baby."

I also didn't want him to know that I was experiencing post-partum depression and I really didn't want to go through the experience of having another baby too soon.

It was thrilling to have a new baby fresh from the realm of God, especially one so healthy and strong. However, I was determined never to have another baby at the Latter-Day Hospital. I had never been treated so badly by doctors before this.

When my doctor didn't show up, the doctor that was assigned to me didn't do anything that I had planned to do with the other doctor. I had asked to not have an episiotomy; they gave me one. I had asked not to be given any drugs to 'help' with the delivery; they gave them to me. I had asked not to be put on a monitor; they stuck it on me anyway.

It was impossible for me to relax and go into my pre-birth trance that I went into with Ann at the Porterville hospital in California. When I could go into the trance, my body would take over with whatever God gave a woman to have a baby naturally, and I felt no pain and very little discomfort.

With this delivery and the way I was treated, it upset me a lot. All control was taken away from me and I was not considered the important part in the birthing process. It was my baby and I wanted it to be born the way I wanted. Apparently, the mom's wishes were not important at the LDS hospital.

Before George was born, Kyle and I gave a big birthday party for Ann. She turned 4 years old. Her birthday is on the 15th of July, we gave her the party on the 16th. We invited all of my cousins and their children to the party. Ann had a blast. Of course, I was ready to pop and pop I did exactly one week later.

August 1, 1976

Today, George Washington L. was blessed. Kyle stumbled a little with the blessing. Seeing how this was his first blessing, he was still a novice. He almost called him Jesus at one point in the blessing, but quickly corrected himself.

Things changed so dramatically in Kyle after George's birth that it was almost as if he discovered and newfound purpose in life.

"I'm going into computers," he stated to me one day clear out of the blue.

"Are you sure about this decision?" I answered. I tried not to be too surprised, but actually I was quite used to his ways of doing things. We had gone through so many changes just that year that I could barely keep up.

"I have never been surer about anything in my life," he replied emphatically.

"I will need to quit my job at Blue Cross so I can study how to become a programmer. I will also get every issue of Byte and Personal Computer magazines I can get," he continued.

"What are we going to do for money?" I inquired. I was somewhat concerned about this new announcement because, after all, I did have a family to feed.

"We will go on Church Welfare for a while," he stated as though this plan would work.

"Church Welfare," I thought to myself. My grandma and I had worked for the Church Welfare System as a secretary and she worked in the meat department at Welfare Square. We were paid in food and clothing and that was all we received for our labors. It was a great experience, but experience does not pay the bills. It made me wonder how the Church was going to do all of this for us.

Apparently the Bishop and he had worked out an arrangement for all expenses to be paid along with having an abundance of food on the table. This Church does not skimp on the food, which was good so I could feed our family well.

Kyle literally locked himself in his office that we had made for him and studied how to become a programmer night and day. There were no breaks, not much socializing with me or the children, and eating a sleeping weren't important either. I made sure he did eat, however. When he finally emerged from his office, he went looking for computer programming jobs and found one with a W. Cleon Skousen in Provo. This man is a noted Historian in the Church and a Politician for less government and what is right in the Constitution. This made me very happy to see Kyle get a job with good pay and with such a good man.

George is now four and one-half months old and is such a strong and intelligent baby. He started getting up off his belly at three and one-half months. He also gets around well in his walker. He loves to scoot wherever Ann is and he loves to pick on the cats. They have already learned to hide to avoid having their hair pulled.

Ann has learned how to write her name and helps me with George. She helps me with the cooking and cleaning of the house. She has a few problems minding me, sometimes, but is very sweet when she wants to be. I love my little family dearly.

Kyle's new job as manager of the Liberty Amendment Committee in Provo keeps him very busy. He is programming all of the programs and running all of the computers. Because of the long drive from South Jordan to south Provo, a distance of about 70 miles, we have stayed a lot at his mother's house.

Oh, I forgot to tell you. Kyle's mother and father retired from their respective jobs in Panama and returned to their very lovely home in Provo. His father was the Chief Electrical Engineer for the Panama Canal Company and his mother worked at the mental hospital that the government provided. They are such lovely people. I really think I will like them. They were enthralled by Ann and Ann loved them right off. Of course, they were thrilled by George, Kyle's first baby.

I did miss my house in South Jordan and let Kyle know I wasn't going to live with his parents. I did not need a repeat of what happened to me when I moved in with Vince's parents. My mother had warned me that if I did, I would lose my husband. Her prophesy came to pass and I did not want it to happen again.

I told Kyle my concerns, and he listened. We sold the house in South Jordan and got an apartment that belonged to Brother Skousen. I happened to be right next to Skousen's son and his family. It was a nice apartment, but I missed my yard and fruit trees and cats. At least Ann had another little girl her age to play with and was thrilled with that fact. She had complained a lot while we were in South Jordan that she had no one to play with. Indeed, we were quite isolated and the only neighbors had teenage sons.

Vince served us papers to take us to court and get Ann from me. After much prayer and consideration as to what to do about this matter, Kyle's father, Keith paid for us to go a Marriage Counselor and then paid the marriage counselor's way to the California court to testify for us. It was a good thing, too. The lawyers we had were no match for Vince's sharp lawyers. They had a script of one lawyer taking the stand while their other lawyer asked him questions as a witness.

What the one lawyer had witnessed was me giving Ann a strawberry on a fork while I was distressfully signing divorce papers at the divorce party they were giving in my behalf. She was old enough to crawl at that time and was crawling under the table when I gave it to her. This was one of the reasons why they were saying I was unfit. The other reason was, I took naps in the afternoon while I was pregnant with Ann. I couldn't believe what they were coming up with to accuse me of being unfit to raise my daughter.

However, my lawyers were stumbling over their questions and didn't know what to ask or retort in return of my defense. So when the Marriage Counselor got up and testified and had a chart and a picture of what Ann drew of who she considered her family, which was Kyle, George and myself, the Judge listened and awarded me full custody. He did award Vince visiting rights of half the summers and some holidays to see Ann. When we explained to Ann about the visiting rights, she wasn't too happy about it, but was willing to do what she had to do.

While Kyle and I were going to counseling, the Counselor made some startling revelations to us about our relationship. He stated that I was a masochist with traits of a martyr, and Kyle was a Sadist. I did not know much about S&M relationships at the time, but the counselor stated that this kind of relationship never gets better, only worse. I later found out that it was called "The burning bed syndrome." Of course the counselor didn't say this in the court because it was not about us, it was about Ann.

Chapter 15

My Writing Dream

Sunday, January 16, 1977
Dear Journal,

We are getting adjusted to our move to Skousen's duplex. George is crawling great and Ann is enjoying her little friend next door.

This last Saturday night, I had a strange dream that woke me up. I dreamed that I became a writer and was writing the story of my life. I went to a publisher and took my journal and they hired me to write the story of my life. My story made lots of money and I bought a yellow house on a hill with a piece of property to go with it.

I also dreamed that needed to continue to go college and take courses of how to write and to improve my vocabulary, but not so much that my diction would go right over people's heads.

I found a lump in my breast tonight. I was so distraught and worried about it because a good share of my Grandma's sisters died of breast cancer. I went to the doctor as soon as I could. He stated that I didn't have anything to worry about. It was just a lump formed by some dry milk that had settled in my breast. This was such relieving news.

I dearly love to nurse and my babies seem to thrive on my milk. My first mother-in-law used to tell me my breasts were too small to have enough milk to feed my baby. This upset me and caused my baby, Ann to be upset also. I nursed her for one year. While I am nursing, my breasts are much larger than their normal size, so this helps my self esteem. Besides, Kyle loves to suck the milk from them, also, which I find a little amusing. It's like I have two babies to nurse. He doesn't do this a lot, but it does bring us closer together. There is a deep bond that happens when a mother nurses her infant.

Friday, February 26, 1977
Dear Journal,

I've procrastinated long enough from writing my history! My husband and I came to the conclusion that I get involved in other people's personal lives and don't concentrate on my own.

George is cutting his first tooth and is miserable. His bottom is also red tonight from the tooth cutting experience.

We enrolled Ann in dance classes a few weeks ago. The teacher has already mentioned that she is a natural dancer. She's such a beautiful and wonderful little girl. She spends a good portion of her day playing the children next door. Yesterday, I started teaching her how to read.

Two weeks ago, the Relief Society gave a lesson about how important it was to send your children on a mission and it was never to young to prepare them for one. I told Ann about the lesson and she said, "I want to go on a mission."

"If you want to save enough money to go a mission, then I will pay a dollar each week to do your chores of making your bed and cleaning your room," I replied.

"Okay!" was her enthusiastic reply. Then she gaily sang to herself, "I'm going on a mission . . .I'm going on a mission . . .I'm going on a mission . . ."

My heart melted as I watched her make her bed and clean her room. She helped me wherever she could. She is such a good little helper.

This mission thing had me pondering about why none of our family had gone on missions. My mother and most of her brothers and sisters all went on missions for the Church. Perhaps it was the family and the father. Her father was a very nice man with a jovial attitude. Her mother was a hard working woman that put herself through school after raising 10 children. Was it because our father was such an abusive man that all we could think of to get away from his beatings at young ages was to get married or join the service? My only brother ended up in mental hospitals because of the abuse. My father didn't want him around after he got big enough to defend himself. It was no wonder none of us went on missions. It takes a strong, loving family to produce missionaries. I hope I can have one.

We were tired of living in the Skousen's duplex and Kyle was beginning to not get along with Skousen's son-in-law. We were looking to move into one of Kyle's brother's houses or one of his parent's many houses. All of them had many houses in Provo that they owned. None of them had a vacancy at this time. We went looking for houses and found one behind the Freeman Institute. We couldn't find out who it belonged to, until a friend of ours informed us that it belonged to the Institute. They wanted $5,000 for the gutted house and the property. It would have been a major fixer-upper, but I have become quite accustomed to them.

At this time, we don't have that kind of cash and we're still waiting for our house in South Jordan to sell. We found a company will to buy the house for our equity. I hop we can get $7,000 for it. Then we could buy the house and property and have a little left for fixing it up.

Lately, I've been going to the temple at least once a week. I go early in the morning while Kyle is watching the children and get back in time for him to go to work. He and I have been discussing the Adam-God theory. We have come to some conclusions that what happened to Adam and Eve in the Garden of Eden would happen to us, too. After all, if we are to help create and start other worlds we would have to do the same thing as they did. I like to joke and say, "What if Adam took the fruit first instead of Eve; would that make men subject to women?" I don't think many men like to think about that possibility since this is such a male dominated society, so I keep this thought to myself much of the time.

I just took Ann to the dentist. He found two cavities on one side of her mouth and one tooth needed a root canal on the other side. It was amazing to me to have my daughter have so many cavities. I never had a cavity in my life. She finally admitted to sneaking money out of the money jar and buying candy at the store around the corner. She said she would quit doing it after this happened.

As a family, we have a family day besides Monday family home evening. Our selected day is Thursday. One Thursday, we went to the park and played with the kids. They loved that. Another day, we went to the drive-in to watch "Rocky." Another Thursday, we went to Ream's Market and got ten hot dogs for $1.00 and four ice cream cones for $0.40. We then would go up to 'Cita's' and Grandpa Lane's house and watch T.V. on their large color screen with their satellite.

One Thursday, we went to my Grandma Nelson's house to visit my mother and sisters. My mother had separated from my father at the advice of a Mormon family counselor after my brother had been in and out of the mental health clinic in Porterville. He told her she had nothing left of her self esteem after my father had abused her and their children those many years. So, she was living in Salt Lake City looking for a job as a secretary for the government. She landed a very good job after a while. At this time, all my family there all had strep throats. My mother seemed to be especially sick, but seemed to be in good spirits in spite of her sickness.

Chapter 16
Fresh Ground

Sunday, February 28, 1977
Dear Journal,

I had a dream last night about someone bombing us. We were either being seized by ex-Mormons or some other country. I couldn't tell. In the dream, I somehow rushed my children home and hide in our basement with all of our supplies. We were able to survive the terrible ordeal because of our supplies.

This dream inspired me to gather all of Kyle's available family, Guy, his brother and his Mom and Dad and inventory all the supplies we had on hand. Our Family Home Evening was very successful in doing this. I want all of our family to be saved together if something devastating happens such as my dream.

Wednesday, March 3rd,

Today went quite smoothly since taking my husband's advice of reading the scriptures and praying first before starting my day.

Kyle just went and bought another Ford Cortina. This one is a blue four door sedan that he paid $75 for. A cop gave him a ticket for not having the tags on it. Kyle paid the ticket and fixed the electrical problems that it had all in one day. Poor man, he nearly froze to death while fixing the car. It snowed while he was fixing it.

We were rejoicing about the snow at the same time because this was an answer to our prayers on the drought that was plaguing Utah at the time. He now has a computer meeting he needs to attend.

March 15th, 1977

Today is Sunday and it is raining. Thank you, Lord! We went to Stake Conference and learned about having music in our homes. Then we came home and a quick lunch. George is so cute and getting quite inventive. He plays peek-a-boo with us by putting a blanket over his head. When he pulls the blanket off, we say boo! He laughs and laughs and thinks it is so funny. He also manages to get on top of the table and starts complaining when he can't come down. He then petitions one of us to take down from the table.

Ann is really getting good with her numbers and most of her alphabet. She is a very smart little girl and will do well in school.

Both of my children are incredibly beautiful.

I was assigned the Targeteer A class in primary and was sustained today. I went Tuesday to see what the class would be like and it looks as if they are a wild bunch of kids. They are nine years old. They proved to be a very challenging class to teach.

Thursday, May 12th, 1977

Kyle, the children and myself went over to 'Cita's' and Keith's house to grind some flour. They purchased a very nice stone grinder and I thought it would be very nice to have some "fresh ground flour" to make some whole wheat bread. Instead of a short sweet visit, Kyle and I began a discussion about how to discipline the children. It all started with Ann and how I shouldn't spank her without warning her first and then teaching her about what she did wrong and how to make it right the next time. I would then reward them if the children did good things and punish them if they messed up. He pointed out that this was the principal of free agency. Without agency, we wouldn't be here. This was the most valuable aspect of God's plan in the pre-existence and why we chose Jesus to come down and die for our agency with his plan instead of Satan's plan that would force us to right and we would have no free agency.

This was so different from the way I was raised. My father was the dictator and we were beat like slaves if we didn't do exactly as we were told. We were never taught about any agency, especially free.

Kyle and I stayed up talking about this until three a.m. in the morning and stayed overnight at 'Cita's and Keith's house and didn't even get home until the next afternoon.

When I finally got home to make the bread, it turned out awful. It was very gritty and did not taste good - so much for "fresh ground" flour for making bread.

My brother, Joe, and sister Darleen, were visiting us before Ann had to go to California to visit her Dad. Joe was recently bailed out of jail by my Mom because my Dad pressed charges on him. Before Ann left, we had the Elders come over and give us all blessings.

My blessing was that I will be able to endure all that will be put on my shoulders with Ann gone and, also, to obey the commandments of the Lord and my husband.

Ann's blessing was that she will be blessed beyond her years to deal with what she has to go through. Satan will be sealed from her. The Holy Ghost will guide her through her life. The Holy Ghost will guide her through her life. She was told to go with those who put Jesus into their life and dear to their hearts and to follow and hold dear the teachings of Jesus.

Kyle's blessing was; the Lord loves and is mindful of you. Nothing comes without much thought and work. Be at rest and follow the Lord's guidance and all will turn out all right. His decisions will leave the forces of the adversary reeling in righteousness.

Joe's was; he must find out about himself and learn to be closer to the Lord. By doing this, he will come to find out about his great mission here on earth and also how important he was before coming here to this earth. If he starts to work for his independence, he will be successful. He will pass through this world with honors. His rough past and future will humble him.

Chapter 17

Cortinas and Death

Wednesday, June 15, 1977
Dear Journal,

A few things have happened since I have last written. Ann went to visit her father on May 28th. She has been there for almost three weeks. I call her once a week. The first week I had to talk to Vince. He was nothing but rude and harassed me. When he finally let Ann talk to me, I asked how she was doing. "I'm doing fine," she answered. I could tell she wasn't to very happy. Then she stated she wanted to come home. I explained to her she couldn't come home for a little while because of the court order. She tried to understand which was probably difficult for a little soon to be five year old.

Last Friday, when I called her, I called person to person for Ann so I wouldn't get any interference from Vince. She talked to me for a while and then started crying about coming home. I explained to her that I could not bring her home at this time. I told her Vince was now in charge of her and she would have to ask them if she could come back home. She was happy with this and promptly ran to ask her Dad if she could go home. Vince got on the phone and said, "We seem to have a problem here."

I told him that if he wanted to talk to me, he could go through his lawyer or call on his own dime. Of course, he did neither. But it bothered me that I was not able to talk to Ann and say goodbye to her.

Kyle and I went to the annual Kennard Family Reunion held in the famous Logan Canyon. We pitched our tent and had a good night's sleep. We played baseball the next day. I hit a homerun. We hiked around the beautiful canyon. George seemed to enjoy himself immensely.

Last week on Friday, Kyle's Grandma died. I was so happy to know her for the small amount of time I did have with her. She was a very intelligent, sweet and wonderful woman. She had fallen and broke her hip and never recovered from the fall. The last time we visited her, I had a feeling she didn't have long to live. The Monday before she died, we took George with us to visit her. She played with him a little and held his foot. Her breathing was raspy like a death rattle. She wouldn't eat anything or drink much. I got her a baby training cup to help her drink, but that didn't help either.

Tuesday was her funeral. It had to be the worst day for Kyle and myself in a long time. We were at each other's throat most of the day for some dumb reason or other. About three a.m. that morning we were both exhausted and finally fell asleep.

The next day, when we went to go to the funeral in the blue Cortina, it wouldn't start. It usually started right up. Today looked like it was an exception. We ended up having to take the purple Cortina station wagon. It started right up. We were on our way to Lehi and then to Richfield where the funeral was going to be held when the purple 'bomb' gave out. Kyle managed to get into the carburetor and find out that floater had disconnected itself. Hence, the reason it flooded. He took the part out and went over to the service station to see if he could get it welded back on . . . or not. Before he left, he told me to be on the look out for any of his relatives that might pass by. I thought this was a strange request, but I looked anyway.

I was sitting in the back of the hatchback and looked for traffic coming. Not too much later, Guy and his family drove up and stopped. Kyle and he talked and Guy asked Kyle if he could be the pall bearer instead of Kyle. Kyle unselfishly let him do this, he was glad to let Guy do the honors. The whole incident was a little strange and we know the Lord had a hand in this matter.

Chapter 18

Premonition

Sunday, October 23, 1977
Dear Journal,

It's been a long time since I last wrote to you. Ann is in a school called "Challenger." We found enough money in our budget to put her in a private school. This school was considered to be a very good school for advanced thinkers like Ann.

George is growing very fast and is learning everything that a baby can learn; he is walking and saying little words such as "Mama," "Dadda," and "Anna".

I am five months pregnant and due around January of 1978. I have kept myself busy watching the children, cleaning house, cooking and being a general "domestic." I need to pride myself for being the perfect "Mormon" wife, also. I was perpetually barefoot and pregnant and letting my "priesthood holder" husband support the family. One thing for sure, I didn't make a "good Catholic" wife.

Kyle spends most of his waking hours at the Freeman Institute and has had two raises in his pay. Of course, this has made us a little richer in our funds for food and miscellaneous items that we could not afford before. I was actually allowed to go buy some new clothing for the children and myself.

Our growing family moved into the basement apartment of one of Kyle's parents' rentals. It has a large back yard with a fence, three bedrooms, albeit one of the bedrooms doesn't have a window, a teensy little kitchen that barely one person can fit into and one bathroom with a shower. The color of the entire basement is bright yellow and is dubbed "The Yellow

Submarine," by Kyle's mother in honor of the Beatle's song by the same name. Who can complain, at least it is a cheerful color for a basement apartment and it is big enough for our growing family at this time.

A good female friend of Kyle's brother, Guy, is moving in upstairs. Her name is Alma. She is from Honduras, Central America. She is a very tall, beautiful woman, and has two pre-teen daughters named Brenda and Lisa. They are proving to be very good upstairs neighbors. They simply adore Ann and she loves their attention. They are also Mormons and strictly adhere to the Mormon standards.

This is so much better that the past upstairs neighbors that recently moved out. The woman ran around the bars of Provo, which I didn't even know Provo or any Mormon town had bars, chasing after men and neglecting her children. Her poor children had to fend for themselves, and looked as if they never had a bath. Their hair was all matted and uncombed, they never had a good cooked meal, the family was always screaming at each other and beating each other up. The mother was always smoking and drinking and demeaning her children and bringing strange men around. It was not a good environment for my little children to be around. So, it was a relief when Alma and her two daughters moved in upstairs.

My maiden Aunt Mary, who could never find a man good enough to suit her, finally found a man she could marry. She is 56 years young. She brought her husband around to introduce him to her family. His name is Jack J., and she showed him off to everyone. I must say he is very handsome older man. I'm impressed. She met this man at the Veteran's Hospital in San Diego. He was full-fledged alcoholic, atheist, and a Naval Officer retiree. Mary bragged about having to save him from the gutter several times. She served him drugs on his food which made him sick every time he would drink, converted him to the Lord and Mormonism. He joined the Church and married her in the temple. I'm so proud of her! Maybe now she will quit trying to run everybody's life. He was joking about how she follows him down to Tijuana to make sure he didn't drink or smoke or bet on the horses. He said she also follows him around the town of San Diego to make sure he doesn't do the same. They play the cat and mouse game. I haven't heard from Aunt Mary for a while on how to run my business, so she must be preoccupied with him. The poor guy.

I went to visit my brother at the Veterans Hospital in Salt Lake City. He was riding his bike and was almost hit by a mail carrier. He proceeded to beat on the truck and was consequently taken to the Hospital under mental duress. I hate to see my brother in such a bad mental state. I do hope and pray he will get better.

My sister, Judi, who was three months pregnant when she married her husband, Dave, finally delivered her baby at their home in Salt Lake City. They didn't have any insurance, and read all the books on delivering the baby at home. The baby was healthy and was a beautiful six pound baby boy. Mom is currently helping her out with cleaning and cooking while Judi recovers.

I am currently taking a Teacher Development course the Church gives to teachers of Sunday school and Primary. This is to help them improve their teaching skills and I truly feel this is helping me become a better teacher.

A funny little incident happened with Kyle and George. George wasn't very tired, but I wanted him to go to sleep so I could prepare my primary lesson, and I felt that him and his dad could get some bonding time in, so I gave him to Kyle who was already in bed. As usual, Kyle put him in the crook of his arm and proceeded to continue to sleep. Being the curious baby that he was, George was feeling Kyle's mustache, and his ears, nose and face. All at once, I heard a bellow from Kyle, "Carla, come here!"

I rushed in the bedroom as fast as I could to see what the matter was. "Take George away!" he yelled. "He was feeling around my face and all of a sudden, I had his finger sticking up my nose at least his second or third knuckle. You also left me with my glasses on!"

I quickly took George and put him in his bed. I was laughing so hard that I couldn't stop. After laughing a while, Kyle yelled, "Carla, if you don't quit your laughing, I will come after you."

I shut up.

December 18, 1977.

I have had this feeling or premonition not to go to the Provo Hospital to have my baby. I felt that it would be best to have this baby at home like my sister Judi had hers. Kyle though it would be best if I found a doctor that would be willing to deliver a baby at home. I found that the same doctor that had taken care of Ann's bladder problem with herbs was willing to deliver the baby at home for $500. He gave me a list of all the things I would need to do the delivery and told me the baby should be arriving in four weeks.

Somehow I found out he was a polygamist. I couldn't have anything to do with a polygamist! I would be excommunicated from the Church! It didn't matter how good of a Doctor he was; he was a polygamist!

I got my money back from him, and then started looking for a midwife. I had to be very careful because midwives in Utah are put on a blacklist and put in prison if found. I finally found one through a friend of a friend. I will not divulge who she is for fear of her good name and practice in Utah.

She informed me that since I was in my last two weeks before delivery, that she usually doesn't take cases such as mine. We paid her what she asked, and then she made a list of everything she needed us to get in order to have a successful delivery.

I had this funny feeling that there was something wrong with this pregnancy. The fetus had been very active in the first and second trimester but was completely still the third. I knew she wasn't dead as the test proved, but something was wrong. I knew, also, that I couldn't let Provo Hospital deliver the baby for some reason. The Lord was telling me, "No, do not go to Provo Hospital." I listened and obeyed the voice that talked to me.

Chapter 19

Visions

Saturday, March 11, 1978
Dear Journal,

I had a beautiful little girl with a reddish tinged hair yesterday morning at 1:00 a.m. I thought I had better tell you the details of the beautiful experience in detail before I forget any part of it.

I started having labor pains Thursday morning about 5 a.m. and had them all day. I managed to do my housecleaning and cooking in between the labor pains. While George was asleep, everything was okay, but when he was awake, he was cranky after his nap and I didn't feel I could handle him. I called 'Cita' to come over and get Ann and George to stay overnight at her home. Of course, Ann was a wonderful little girl and helped around the house and played with her friends for a while. I just felt the two of them should be elsewhere while I had the baby.

George had been acting really strange for the past week or so, almost as if he knew something was going to happen. He would wake up to or three times a night and would cry for me and cling to me as if he were never going to see me again. Alma called this action 'cipe', a Spanish name for when a baby knows something is going to happen. She explained that her Indian ancestry knew that little babies intuitively knew something was going to happen.

We had pulled Ann out of the private school because she just wasn't adjusting to it. She would go hide behind the door or in the bathroom and not want to come out and participate with the other children. So we decided to enroll her in the public school down the street from us. She blossomed in this school. She loved to play with her friends at school and loved her teacher. She had brought her first little book home from school and was so excited that she could read it. She excitedly exclaimed, "Now I can read you to sleep, Mommy!" Then she went around reading it to everyone in the house as many times as she could.

After the children were gone, I called Kyle at work about 3:30 p.m. to come home and be with me. Gary, a good friend of ours, had given me a book called, "Husband Coached Childbirth." I started reading it to Kyle and then asked Kyle to read it. He got another book from Gary and was reading it, also.

When he arrived at the basement apartment, I was pretty well into my contractions. Since we decided to have this baby at home, there was no mad rush to the hospital for all the red tape. We called the midwife to let her know about my contractions and she informed us that she would be on her way. I had since moved from my favorite green Lane reclining chair that I had salvaged from my first marriage, to the converted bed/couch that I had bought beautiful flowered discontinued upholstery material and sewed covers around some foam pillows and a coverlet around the bed. Since my contractions had started, this bed/couch was converted to a delivery bed.

All the necessary items that were needed for the delivery were gathered together and accounted for, and we both made ourselves comfortable to wait for the arrival of our baby. I already knew this baby was going to be a girl. The Lord had informed me of this fact, so we had already chosen the name Merri Ly for her. With this already taken care of, we started to talk.

Kyle was very knowledgeable about gospel doctrine of his previous life before he came to this earth. He was told in his Patriarchal Blessing that he was so great in his previous life that his memory of the Plan of Salvation could not be blotted out. He began telling me it was harder for the baby to come into this world than for me to bring it here, because it was leaving the light of our Father in Heaven. Coming into this cold and dreary world was not easy. It was necessary for my spirit and body to pass into the valley of the shadow of death to be able to show her that I would be willing to go through some pain to bring her into this world. This would make her feel that I loved her more than anything in the world and then the great pain of leaving her Father in Heaven would be more bearable.

Kyle and I passed the time by talking a lot about the things of God. Things I had never contemplated during my entire life. We talked about many other things which I can't remember at this time. What really mattered was that he and I and the Lord were very close to each other in the spirit and the Spirit of the Holy Ghost and we were feeling very good. I could feel the spirit move upon me and I could peacefully get to the business of having our baby.

After talking about the book that our friend gave us to use during the delivery, we decided that it was written by a man led by the knowledge of men, so we put it aside and let the spirit guide us. The man was suggesting all kinds of busy work to keep the mother's mind off her pain. I found that with my knowledge of birth learned by Kyle, that I welcomed each contraction with joy and as I was farther and farther along, I was so intensely relaxed, that my body was like lead and my spirit was quite free to explore unseen things and feelings.

Kyle called the midwife around 6:30 p.m., she decided that I had a while to go still before the baby came, and she had a fifteen year old daughter that was six months pregnant from a stranger that had slipped a micky in her drink and had raped her while she was out cold. She had awakened to him zipping up his pants and found her own down. Not knowing quite what had happened, she had found herself pregnant and decided to let her mom keep the baby after it was born. She was going to continue her schooling as a regular person and keep on living her life. I admired the young girl for her bravery and was happy that she could see through her pregnancy without wanting to get an abortion. The midwife wanted her to observe how peaceful I was during my contractions so she could get an idea of how to go through with them when her time came. She also wanted her to see how wonderful a birthing could be between a husband and a wife. She then gave me some comfrey tea and some red raspberry leaf tea to help in my delivery.

The midwife and her daughter were wondering how Kyle and I were having such a good time with the delivery. Kyle read some of Orson Pratt's book, "The Seer," which fell right to the page he wanted about 'The Plan of Salvation." Kyle then tried to explain some of the doctrine to them and how this was helping us in the delivery. Being Mormons, they understood some of it, but most of it went right over their heads. They couldn't fathom how this would help in the delivery of a baby.

After a while of this conversation, the midwife decided it was time to take her daughter home.

While she was gone, I experienced a magnificent vision. The wall I was next to opened up to a vast, beautiful blue expanse of what appeared to be heaven. It was so glorious! I saw people coming toward me in what appeared to be my spirit bed. I saw three boys that were so glorious and bright that I could hardly look upon them. They were stair-stepped from the tallest to the shortest. The tallest one appeared to be the oldest and was the first one to talk to me in the spirit. When you talk in the spirit, I found, you talk from your forehead and thoughts. They were gathered around my spirit bed and seemed sad about losing their sister to the world. When I began to talk to them in the spirit, they seemed to cheer up.

While I was seeing this vision, I was telling Kyle about it. He couldn't see what I saw, so I described everything in detail that I was seeing in the spirit. He seemed to know that the three boys that were gathered around my spirit bed were my future children and they were saying goodbye to their sister that was coming into this world. Kyle wanted me to ask them what they wanted to be named when they were born in this world.

The oldest and the tallest of the three answered first to my spiritual inquiry. He told me that he wanted to be named Benjamin Franklin L. I then looked at the middle one and began speaking to him in the spirit. I asked him what he wanted to be named. He stated in the spirit that he would like to be named Kyrt Patrick L. The shortest one wanted to be named John. I asked him if I could name him John Quincy Adams since he was a direct ancestor of ours, and he agreed. Their spirits were so brilliant; they looked like they were part of the sun. They seemed very happy to be able to talk to me.

Then other spirits came around my bed to talk to me. I recognized my Grandpa Eggman, Grandpa Nelson, and a whole bunch of others who apparently were my ancestors that had passed on before in this life. My attention was particularly drawn to my Grandpa Eggman. He looked sad. I couldn't believe anyone would be sad in such a glorious place as what I was envisioning, I also couldn't hardly believe he was in this beautiful place. After all the years of 'Mom-Judy' saying in detail all the bad things he had done to her, and the stories of his boozing, womanizing and gambling that I heard from both my father and my grandmother, I thought for sure he would not be in this beautiful place of Heaven that I was seeing. But he was there and not in Hell where I thought he would be. I was wondering if he was such a bad man, how did he make it to Heaven? I asked him why he was sad. He answered that his wife, Judy, didn't want anything to do with him when she died.

Man! Did I know what he was talking about! After years of listening to her, I knew just how he felt. I told Kyle what he said to me. Kyle had me apologize for the way my Grandmother was and told me to tell him not to worry about it. Everything would turn out okay.

This seemed to make him very happy. He also asked me about my Dad's temple work. I informed him that Dad was working very hard on his names to get them into the temple and have the family be sealed. He then seemed very happy and went on his way.

All the spirits seemed to be very busy to talk very much and had to be on their ways to do their business. After a while all the other spirits left and the three bright spirit children remained around the bed and finished saying their goodbyes to their sister.

Little did I know that they would never see her in this earthly life.

After the vision, the birthing process began in earnest. The midwife had come back and was worried that Merri Ly was not progressing properly through my birth canal. We waited and waited. I pushed and pushed. She just wouldn't come down the canal. Finally, in one last five minute shove, she came out. She was blue and wasn't breathing. He had her umbilical cord wrapped twice around her neck and once around her arm and it was also short.

It was touch and go from there on out. We placed her on my belly and worked on her feet and massaging her lungs. Because of her short cord, my placenta had been yanked out of my womb sooner than it should have been, and I began gushing blood. Everything that had been planned for to stop the bleeding, such as ice and kneading my stomach, was not stopping the profusion of blood escaping from my body. Everything was in a frenzy. Merri Ly needed to start breathing, and I needed to stop gushing blood.

The midwife was frantic. After a few minutes, Merri Ly started to cry and her color started to get pink. Kyle had dashed up to the stairs and awakened Alma, frantically asking for anything to save my life. (I found out about this from Alma years later.) She promptly said a little prayer and then remembered an herb from her Indian grandmother that would stop my bleeding. She hurried and made the Cayenne Pepper tea and Kyle then rushed it down to me and yelled, "Here drink this!"

"Yaaah!" I yelled, not expecting something so hot and spicy. I was promptly jerked out of my pre-comatic state that I was in because of the great loss of blood that I experienced and I immediately stopped my bleeding.

It was like a major miracle that both Merri Ly and I were both alive.

We were all relieved that this ordeal was over. The placenta was later buried in our back yard. Alma explained this was good for the ground and for the spirits.

Both the baby and myself quickly mended. She is such a beautiful little girl with her strawberry red hair and happy smile.

As for my premonitions about going to Provo Hospital, my Mom's sister, Joan, came to me one day and told me a scary story. She told me about a woman that had come to her in the Oakland temple crying on her shoulders that her doctor son was playing God in the Provo Hospital and decided which baby lived and which baby didn't. I then talked with a cousin about another incident about a woman in the LDS hospital having a baby where the woman had also had a short placenta and was hemorrhaging profusely and the baby was not breathing. They forgot about the baby and concentrated on saving her. The baby died and woman almost died.

I then had the opportunity to talk with a woman about her experience when her son who was retarded was born. She was in my grandmother's ward and I got to see this woman quite often, so we knew each other. She had the same thing happen to her as my experience. They had put the baby in an incubator with too much oxygen and by the time they got her bleeding stopped and checked the baby, it was too late. His brain was already damaged from the oxygen. Her husband blamed her for the baby's retardation and left her.

My premonitions and spiritual guidance had prompted me to do what I knew I needed to do. Everything turned out in the delivery and God and my dear friend, Alma and my husband and with the help of the midwife saved Merri Ly's and my life.

Merri Ly is a good name for her. She is such a happy beautiful baby. Her little eyes light up whenever we sing the song, "Merrily We Roll Along," to her. We sing it a lot to her.

Chapter 20

Late Great Planet

April 28, 1978
Dear Journal,

We had a "Goodbye" party for Kyle. He is going to Europe and Israel for three weeks with W. Kleon Skousen as a gofer. I would like to go too, but Merri Ly is much too young to leave and I don't have $2,400. Kyle and I worked hard getting everything that he would need to take with him on this fabulous trip. We packed everything, including his red, white, and blue plaid sports jacket that he was so proud of and loved to wear. After the three weeks, he came back without it. After asking where it was, he answered, "A man in Egypt was so enamored by the jacket, that I just gave it to him." I was proud of his generosity.

Curious about his trip, I asked what Egypt was like. He stated that it was the filthiest country he had ever seen. The people have their bowel movements right in the streets and the river Nile is so polluted that if you touch it, you will die.

I then asked what Israel was like. He stated that it was the cleanest city he had ever been in. He stated everything was pristine white and spotless. Someday, I want to visit both places.

Tuesday, May 2, 1978

Yesterday, I took Merri Ly and Ann to the doctor. Merri Ly is 10 pounds and 2 ounces and 22 inches long. She was doing very well since her birth on March 10th. Ann has contracted another bladder infection. I started her on her regimen of antibiotics and lactobacillus-acidophillus, chlorophyll, oat straw tea, and cranberry juice that the Naturalpathic Doctor had instructed me to do. Yes, this was the same doctor that was also the polygamist. I didn't care. His regimen worked and kept her clear of her bladder infections. This was much better than putting her under the knife to replace her leaking urethra and have her wear a diaper for the rest of her life. I also made sure that she didn't take bubble baths and taught her how to wipe herself from front to back. She also couldn't wear nylon panties, only cotton.

I had my lawyer, Ana Garland, write this information to Vince when Ann would go to see him on her next visit.

We then visited my Mom at my Grandma Nelson's house Friday night over the weekend. My Mom had applied for and landed a very good government job as a Personnel Director in Salt Lake City, and now she was transferring to a Federal Government job as a Personnel Director in Taft, California. She had stayed in Salt Lake City for two years and had a greater self-esteem than I had seen in years. I was happy for her and my sisters and brother. They were doing very well in Salt Lake City. Even my brother had gone to upholstery school in Salt Lake City and was doing well and talking of setting up his own upholstery business.

Mom was worried that my father was going to give away the farm to a woman that he had moved into her home to take care of the place, so she wanted to go home. She had enough spunk to stand up to my Dad now and not take his abuse, but I was worried about my sisters and brother.

I was hoping my brother would stay away from my father, and fulfill his dream, but he decided to go back. I hope and pray everything will go all right for my family when they return.

Saturday, June 10th, 1978

Kyle and I spent the whole day together. It was the first time in a long while that we had any time together. He had come back from the Middle East with the stories that I previously mentioned.

We then worked on our finances and found out just where we were. We then got ready to go the deposition on child support from Vince. With Kyle's clear thinking and state of mind the deposition went very well.

After that, we went to the park and had a picnic. We were supposed to meet some people from our Church there, but we didn't see them until we were finished eating. We had to go and turn on the water at Kyle's parents' home.

After the watering was finished, Kyle suggested that we go to a movie that one of his friends at work suggested we go to called, "The Late Great Planet Earth." We went. It was a superb movie on all the prophecies in the Bible on modern times from John the Revelator and the Old Testament Prophecies of Daniel, Ezekial and other prophets of the Bible. It was narrated by Orson Welles. The movie literally left me shaking in my boots. It graphically told about Gog and Magog and what they were going to do about Israel. It was terrible to see it happen on screen. It will be even worse in real life.

It talked about in 1982, there will be the Jupiter effect where all the planets will line up. This will cause the sun to do strange things. Dead volcanos will erupt all over, the ozone layer will be disturbed and people will get more skin cancer. The earth will be more like a woman just about ready to have a baby. More hurricanes, tornados, earthquakes, and other natural disasters such as earthquakes in diverse places will happen so intensely and increase in number so fast, that it will be like the earth is in travail of child labor just like the Bible stated.

The move also mentioned the Anti-Christ's numbers of 666 in his name and everyone who wanted to buy and sell would have to have it in their hands or forehead. The Anti-Christ would be raised by the power of Satan from the dead. Everyone who put the numbers 666 in their forehead and be the Anti-Christ's followers are enemies of the true Christ. The Anti-Christ would say there would be peace, and there would be peace for seven years. Then the whole world would turn against Israel and be gathered against her. Then Christ would come down and split the Mount of Olives in half. The remaining people who were alive in Israel would rush out to see their 'Savior' and wonder who he was. They would see his nail prints in his hands and feet and see his sword wound in his side and know then who He was. They would be sorry about not recognizing him as their Messiah and he would forgive them. Those who follow the Anti-Christ would then be burned in the end.

Then the earth will change and become celestialized and Christ will rule the Earth as the Bible stated.

This movie was such an eye opener to me, that I could barely stand up and walk out of the theater, I was shaking so hard.

When we arrived home, we were told by Gloria and Brenda that our prophet Spencer W. Kimball had given the divine Melchezedic Priesthood that the church held sacred to the Blacks. Kyle thinks that the outside world will think that this action by the Brethren was just a smart political move. The Blacks had been threatening to sue the Church for racial discrimination. Since the LDS Church was one of the last Churches not to allow the Blacks in their priesthood order, we were not too surprised about this move by the church. But, we were wondering if it was a divine move or a political move. It did leave some doubts in our minds.

We then read in the paper about India not signing the armaments race agreement. India is having severe famine and might even use nuclear power to get the food that they need.

Today, other than going to the store and getting an EPT or Early Pregnancy Test at the drug store, I didn't do too much. I was thinking I was pregnant again. Fortunately, I was not.

Wednesday, June 14th

I was visiting Francie, Kyle's old friend that I had given up the apartment in the Avenues, when all of a sudden, Jack, her big black dog bit my son George on the mouth hard enough for the skin to break and his lip was bleeding. Francie made the excuse for her dog saying that George ran over the dogs' toe. Just a little while later, while George wasn't even close to the dog, he again bit George on the lip. George really screamed this time. Francie then apologized profusely. I suggested that she put Jack down if he could not be trusted around little children.

Thursday, June 15th

Today, I took George in for a tetanus shot and called Francie to see if her dog was current for his shots. Jack's next shot is due in August, so he should not have rabies was her reply. I asked her to keep Jack under surveillance for ten days to see if he has rabies or not.

Friday, June 16th

I worked on my sales in Amway today. Of course, I was sold on the idea and the many thousands of money I could make. But I just couldn't get past the idea that I needed to get a lot of people below me to gain more money instead of selling the product. I was raised selling oranges and the more you sold, the more you made.

George is limped today when he walked. He was also a little cranky from the effects of the tetanus shot. He also had a swollen lip from the bite.

Kyle once again seemed to be very diligent in keeping in touch with all of his old college buddies from the U. Of course, Francie was one of his old flames from his "hippie era." She once confided to me that she quit sleeping with Kyle because he would inevitably end up giving her some kind of STD that she didn't need. This revelation made me feel uneasy about my relationship with Kyle. I hoped that I didn't catch anything from him and his earlier 'sexual revolution' days.

Chapter 21
My Father's Stories

Sunday, July 23, 1978

Today, I took it very easy. Friday and Saturday, I had participated, planned and put together a Nelson Family Reunion in Provo Canyon. We were on Granite Flat 'A' on Timpanogos Mountain not far from where Joe C. and I had started when we climbed the mountain just a few years earlier. It was such a wonderful day with lush green pines and the beautiful growth around the camp. Some of the relatives went for a hike to the Timpanogos Cave, some of us played baseball, Ann had a fabulous day playing with her first cousins once removed. She had just arrived from California on the 14th of July and was able to make the reunion. George had a fun time playing with the other two year old cousins, and of course, Merri Ly had fun just playing in the dirt. She is four months old and is already getting up on all fours, like a little puppy dog, and getting around very well. There were thirty-two of us there and we all had a very good time.

After all of us had gone home from the reunion, my Dad and sister, Suzanne, came over. Garlan, my father, started telling us stories he had never told us before.

He told about a time in 1947, before he had met and married Mom, he had bought a brand new truck and worked hard to pay for it by painting houses. He lived in a little shack that didn't cost any rent. "Every time I bent down to get a bucket of paint, my back would go out and I would be in so much pain."

"I would go to a chiropractor and get my back put back in, and then I would get in my truck and my back would pop out again. I would again be in a lot of pain. I would have other painters and the chiropractor pop my back in again. I laid on a board to try to straighten my back out, I tried everything."

He went on with his story, "The Latter-Day-Saint church was then just a mission in California. I had to go clear up to San Francisco to the Mission President if I wanted a Temple Recommend. I went to Church at the branch in Bakersfield and one of the General Authorities happened to be there. He was blessing one lady to get her well, so I figured I would ask him for a blessing to relieve me of my back pain."

"Well, the Apostle did bless me, but he told me something in his blessing that was very strange. He stated that if I ever fell away from the Church of Jesus Christ, I would be in ten times as much pain as I was then."

"I went and painted the next day. I bent down to get the bucket of paint – I had no pain. I drove my truck – I had no pain. I swamped potatoes out of the field, brought them in, unloaded them – I had no pain. I could hardly believe it!"

"For twenty years, I had no pain in my back until I started having trouble with Joe, and then I started working on Sundays because I was getting money crazy. I had worked two Sundays in a row and had bursitis in my arm so bad that I had to lift one arm with my other arm just to get it up. I went to the Veterans' Hospital and they couldn't do anything with it, so I decided that I had better go to church and take the Lords day off. I immediately got better."

This was definitely a testament to Suzanne and myself that the Lord certainly works with people if they follow his commands.

He went on to tell us about another story of when he was about twenty.

"I was in the Pacific Isles during World War II on the USS Enterprise. We hadn't had any supply ships for a long time and all we had to eat was dried potatoes and bologna. We all were so tired of the same thing every day."

"Finally, one day we got leave to go on one of the islands. He search around and got some coconuts, papaya, lemons, nuts that looked like cashews and some bananas. I hoarded them and didn't want to share them with anyone, but it was so hot and humid that they started to spoil. So, I gorged myself on them and got so sick that I was throwing up and had diarrhea so bad, that I couldn't get off the toilet."

"When I finally could get away from the head, I made it down to the mess hall, and the chef had pity on me and gave me three oranges from a new shipment that had come in from a supply ship. I ate them immediately and became well from that moment on."

"Then, I was wondering what had caused me to become so sick and decided to use some of the service boys (those who cleaned the ship) as guinea pigs and gave them some of the nuts and food I had been hoarding. They, too, became sick just like I did. Later, I heard that about fifty sailors were seriously ill because of the nuts and an announcement over the intercom cautioned everyone against eating them."

It was nice to be able to talk to my Dad for the first time in my life. I was used to being yelled at or beaten by him if we didn't do our work around the farm. It was very comforting to know he, too, was also a person – not just my Dad. I'm sure Suzanne felt the same way – even though she had to go back to working with him. I was glad to be able to be out of the household and the craziness that went with it, even though I had my own problems to have to deal with.

George is going through a stage of getting lost around the block. He loves to wander and it's very hard to keep track of him with the new baby. He is able to open the door to our apartment and get out without me knowing. He also likes to sneak up to Alma's upstairs apartment and open her shampoo bottles and watch the slow-moving syrupy shampoo trail down to the drain. She has caught him more than once at this and had to scold him along with me in which he takes great delight in. He also delights in taking all my pots and pans out, lines them up and plays train with them with his little sister, Merri Ly. They have so much fun pounding the pans and playing together.

Ann loves going upstairs to play with Brenda and Gloria. It is so nice to have someone that Ann adores and they are such nice little girls for her to play with. She helps me with making her bed and some of the chores around the house. I hope she gets well from her recurring bladder infections, soon. I don't want to have to get an operation on her ureter.

Chapter 22

Washington, D.C.

Friday, August 11, 1978.

Dear Mom,

Kyle left for Washington, D.C., Wednesday, and should be there by now. He took the Red Cortina bomb and should be there by now. The cleaners made a mistake on his suit and gave him an identical smaller blue suit. I will have them exchange it and send it back to him in D.C.

Merri Ly is crawling around very well at five months. I went to an OB-GYN to find out if I was pregnant again. They said no, I was just fat around the middle.

Joe is doing okay at the V.A. hospital. Since you signed him up in the courts, they now have more power over him than we do our own children. What Joe will have to do is to learn to act sane even if the rest of the world is acting crazy. It's all up to him. As for the prolixin that is destroying his brain, I don't know what to do about it.

George got his hair cut Sunday by Kyle. You won't be able to say 'Georgina' any more to him, but he is still a beautiful baby.

Please send me Maureen's and Teresa's addresses. I'll probably see Maureen in person in Maryland if Kyle quits his job. He is looking for a job back in D.C. He's getting tired of the two-man circus at the Liberty Amendment at Provo.

Ann is doing fine in school and dancing. She loves her neighbors, Brenda and Gloria and enjoyed the visit with Suzanne and Dad.

Kyle seems very determined that we are going to move to Virginia probably in November. He has suggested liquidating my Amway business. He has been campaigning for Jed Richardson and we hope he wins. He might get a job working for him if he wins.

Mom - your idea about taking your job and going part-time and working in the bees sounds good. Let me know what you are going to do.

Dad – Continue treating Mom well and your rewards will keep on coming in from God.

Suzanne – Please write Ann. She would love to get a letter from you and she will write you back. She misses you. How's school and your boyfriends? Whatever happens, stay close to the Lord and the Church.

Darleen – Ann would love it if you would write her, also. You would get a letter back from her. She misses you, too.

I must go now. I miss all of you and hope to see you again, soon.

Love always,
Kyle, Carla, Ann, George and Merri Ly

Dear Journal,
September 2, 1978,

On Sunday, August 18, 1978, I was walking to a Sacrament meeting to see a farewell meeting for a family's daughter who was going on a mission. I had all three children in my little wagon going down the block. The church was only a block and a half distance from our apartment. I noticed there was a pretty blond lady following behind us with a little boy holding her hand. "She looks lonely," I thought, "I wonder if she is new around here?" I stopped my little procession and addressed her. "Hi!" I said.

She flashed a big beautiful smile at me and said, "Hi!" back to me.

I proceeded to introduce myself and all my children in the wagon to her.

She promptly introduced me to herself, "Debbie is my name and this is Christian or Chris. He is my son."

She was impressed with my children, quickly learned all of their names, and was really taken by Merri Ly's big dimples and smile. She promptly wanted to hold her and play with her. "What a beautiful little baby," she exclaimed. Merri Ly instantly fell in love with her.

We started talking about her life. "I have been a member of the Mormon church for two months. I came out here from Duluth, Minnesota with a lady who did jewelry. She brought me out here to watch her kids ranging from 18, 16, & 15. The 18 year old resents me being his babysitter."

"Isn't he a little old for a babysitter?" I quipped.

Her pretty brown eyes flashed when she said, "Yes, and I'm beginning to wonder why I even came. However, the weather is so much better here than in Duluth."

Never being in Duluth, I asked, "What is it like there?"

"It is always so cold and windy, it blows right off the Great Lakes, right through Duluth," she replied.

She was beautiful with bigger breasts than I, of course that is not hard to do with me. I asked if she was married.

"No, I never married," she replied. "As soon as my boyfriend found out I was pregnant, he took off."

"That's the pits," I stated. I thought about a friend of Kyle's named Rick that seemed to be a nice catch for some woman if they could get him. He had joined the Church not to long ago, also. But, I wanted to get to know this wonderfully friendly woman before I started playing match-maker.

"When is your birthday?" I asked, being curious. I always liked to know people's birthdays to know how they would get along with my Scorpio sign.

"It's in July," she replied.

"Oh good," I answered. "That's a very good sign for a Scorpio to get along with." I was happy her and my sign complimented each other.

I also knew that Rick's sign was a Scorpio, and they would get along with each other. "Later," I thought to myself, "I will introduce them."

We went to Church together and sat with each other, I took Sacrament, we both listened to the talks and saw the young woman say her goodbyes before she would go on her two year Mormon mission. It was probably like my Mom's farewell Sacrament meeting before she went on her two year mission to Mexico in 1944.

September 7, 1978.

This morning was Ann's appointment with the Urology Clinic at the Primary Children's Hospital in Salt Lake City. To do the testing, she could not eat or drink from the midnight before until it was all over. When I went to go awaken her that morning, she said in a very sad voice, "Mommy, I don't want to go take the test. I already took the test in California when I was at my Daddy's house and it hurt to take the test."

I was shocked! This is the first time I had heard about this. Wanting to know more about what she just informed me of, I called Sava, her grand-mother to ask why I wasn't told about this fact.

She said, "You need to call Vince's wife, Helena, about it. Here is the number."

Helena, when I got hold of her, stated, "Yes, we paid $250 to take her to the hospital for testing and found that her bladder was all right, but Ann needed to learn how to wipe herself and take hot sitz baths every night to wash herself well. She also needed to make sure to take all of her medication and do a culture periodically."

Of course, this made me feel as if they thought I wasn't doing my job as her mother. So, I asked, "Why haven't you told me about this before now?"

Helena answered, "Because of the all the legal red tape that has been set up between me and my uplines' (Vince) commands, I haven't been able to. I'm sorry that I didn't give you the information before now."

While talking to Sava, she stated, "Your basement is too cold, you aren't teaching Ann how to wipe herself, and the pills you are giving her are from a fake doctor or chiropractor and they aren't doing any good for her."

Of course, this running me down was nothing new to me. Ann also informed me that while she was visiting them, all they did was continually run me down telling her what an unfit mother I was to her.

After talking with them, I wasn't quite sure what to do. The conversations with them made me late for the appointment, but felt that it was best to take her anyway. Poor Ann. She cried and hollered because she didn't want to go through the same pain as before when they did the tests in California. "I saw the tubes they put in my bladder, and it hurt, Mommy," she cried. "I don't want to do it, again!"

Trying to empathize with her, but knowing she must go through it again, I had to be strong.

The Primary Children's Hospital was really good for her. They put her to sleep so she wouldn't see or feel anything. They also had her do a puff painting of herself which I hung on my wall. After the testing, she said, "I'm glad they put me to sleep, Mommy. It wasn't as bad as when I was in California."

Of course this made me feel a little better. We went out for ice cream after the testing. This made her feel better.

After getting home, I was able to tell Kyle all about what had happened. He was still in D.C., working hard on the Liberty Amendment. He stated that I needed an eternal viewpoint when looking at things. He was referring to my checkbook balance, but this could apply to anything. "I'm lonely here without you," he stated.

"I'm lonely without you, too," I replied. "The children miss you, and so do I."

"I don't think you should give party plans for your Amway business," he stated. "They are very coercive and put pressure on people to join."

"Okay," I replied. "I'm really not doing too well in the business, anyway. I'm thinking of quitting, as you suggested before."

"Well, goodbye, I love and miss you," he stated. I stated the same.

Debbie, my new friend, got herself an apartment today with the Bishop's help. With my suggestion that she should get out on her own after seeing the reality of her living conditions, the bishop helped her get an apartment. I introduced her to Rick. They hit it off immediately. It appears they might get serious.

Ann is doing well in her dancing lessons. Kyle and I decided to put her in regular school after the teacher would find her hiding behind the door. She didn't want to do the rigorous work they private school had her doing. She loved the Kindergarten in the Utah school system and thrived. She loved all her friends at school and there were more children for her to play with.

Merri Ly is growing so fast and loves playing with pots and pans with George. He seems to love arranging all the pots and pans up and having her come and mess them all up. He takes it all in stride. They entertain themselves by the hour. I hardly have to do anything to interfere with them. It's so nice to have children so close together. Ann would always cry because she didn't have anyone to play with. My mother was right when she stated, "It's better to have children close together, then they can have someone to play or fight with."

November 5, 1978, Sunday night.
Dear Journal,

I feel like my life is on the edge of a cliff. My husband and I know Jed Richardson is going to win, but what we are going to do after the election is what we don't know. We know we are going to go to Washington, we just don't know how we are going to do it.

Kyle had a dream quite a while ago showing that he was called to be first counselor in the first presidency by L. Tom Perry, who is an apostle now.

Friday night, Alma had another dream which was long and she was extremely exhausted when she woke up. She couldn't remember any of it when she awoke. She prayed quickly to the Lord to ask for some memory of her dream. She remembered that she walked into an office with most beautiful desk and the most elaborate office she had ever been in. Kyle was behind the desk in a very well-tailored, blue suit and got up and shook her hand and said, "Well, Alma, I am the Secretary of State."

Alma, being from Honduras, didn't know what Secretary of State was until we explained to her that Henry Kissinger was the Secretary of State at the time. Then she understood her dream.

After note; Jed Richardson lost the election.

Chapter 23

Grandma's Old Brass Bed

Sunday, December 10, 1978.
Dear Journal,

Since Kyle was laid off at the Liberty Amendment, he found another job in Salt Lake City. We moved to a one bedroom apartment about two weeks ago. We are on the second floor and have a very nice view of Salt Lake City from the East side. We can see the State Capitol, the Mormon Temple, and the mountains clear on the West side of the Great Salt Lake Basin. It is quite a change from our basement apartment. The kitchen is big, which was a welcome change from the kitchen in the basement. Two people couldn't even fit in that kitchen. Kyle and I are sleeping on a foldout couch in the front room, while the kid's are all stationed in the one bedroom. The rent is $145 a month.

The people are really nice here, but the kids and I really miss Alma and her kids and I miss Debbie. We were invited to a party after running into one of the tenants on the elevator. The couple's names were Pat and Bent. Pat was a beautiful African-American woman from Minnesota and Bent is from Denmark.

I was carrying groceries up, while struggling with my three children, and Pat offered to help me carry my groceries up the elevator. I guess she thought I had my hands full with three small children and all my bags of groceries. She was right.

I left my children with a babysitter while I was at the party. It was being held just down the hall from our apartment. My other children loved being left with the babysitter, who also happened to be their second cousin, Chrisele's daughter, Shawn. All except Merri Ly. She doesn't seem to want me out of her sight. She clings to me and cries when I leave. She seems to cling to me more that ever now. Not to long ago, we were having dinner with Keith and Lea, Kyles' Mom and Dad. She talked about her little boy, Larry, who died when he was three during a visit to the dentist. She stated that he was into everything, never able to sit still. He would always want to go out to the canal and play around it. She always worried that he would drown in the canal.

"You know," she stated with concern, "Merri Ly reminds me an awful lot like Larry. She never sits still and always seems to look into everything like she has a very short life to live."

I pondered this statement in my heart. I realized that I had never seen another baby quite like her. When we took her to church she was crawling under all the pews. We couldn't keep tabs on her. When we took her to 'Cita's and Grandpa's house, she was into every room, exploring every detail, playing with all the pots and pans, playing with everything she could get her hands on. She was never still. She would sit in my arms long enough to eat, and off she was exploring some more. She was barely nine months almost ten months old. She seemed as though she could not live life fast enough.

At the party, I met a Russian couple. The woman had just arrived the Saturday before. She was extremely beautiful with strawberry blond hair and blue eyes. She was very interested in genealogy in which I was very well versed in since I had helped my Grandma Nelson do hers. I told her about the Mormon Genealogy Library next to Temple Square. I had spent many an hour with my Aunt Joan and Grandmother there. She was interested. She told me that he husband and her had to get divorced so he could migrate here a year ago. He is Jewish. They have one child. The reason why they decided to come to America instead of Jerusalem, is because she is not Jewish and the Jews in Jerusalem would not take to kindly to her being Russian. When I told her how many children I had, she said I was rich.

For some reason, they did not get remarried after she came to America. Her and her former husband were interested in seeing the city and I offered to show it to them. She came over to our apartment and brought her baby with her. I had never seen such a cute, fat baby so bundled up. The poor thing was so bundled, that its little face was beet red. I tried to suggest maybe taking off a few of the warm clothes, but was told the baby was used to being bundled.

Merri Ly and her baby began to take interest in each other and started to play with each other and George and his pots and pans.

Kyle is working at Microcosm selling and programming computers. He gets 8% on whatever he sells. His boss mentioned he could use me to sell computers.

Monday, December 18, 1978.

Dear Journal,

Our family went down to 'Cita's' for the weekend so Kyle could help with the work on their 'pent house' that they are building on the top of their garage. It will be like a very large playroom/bedroom for the guests and their grandchildren. They go down to Deseret Industries for all kinds of the neatest toys and my children love to come and play at their house. It's so wonderful to have in-laws that actually love me and adore their grandchildren. They are treating me with nothing but kindness and are thrilled that their son actually married such a nice person such as myself and is willing to have children by him. It's such a change from my last in-laws that I bask in the light of their love.

One day, while we were visiting 'Cita' and Keith, I sewed a quilt from her scrap pile. It was cloth ends and pieces that she had picked up from a clothing manufacturing place in Orem.

While I was sewing, George found a crayon and proceeded to draw all over 'Cita's' walls. I proceeded to spank him and him and I scrubbed the walls. I explained to him that he needed to draw on paper and not on the walls. I then went back to work making his quilt. He proceeded to draw on the walls again. I had him scrub the walls again. It seems that he has this urge to be an artist. Merri Ly and George then played with 'Cita's' pots and pans. Ann wanted me to play a little game with her. We played for a while. Then I made a pumpkin pie with Ann. It seems that I didn't get too much accomplished today. I did enjoy the time with my children, however.

I don't know what we are going to do for Christmas this year. It's only six more days, I am without a car and don't feel like traveling much with such a large batch of kids. Kyle hasn't been able to sell very many computers, so we are broke.

I had a nightmare last night and woke up in a cold sweat it was so real. I told Kyle about it because it was so real I needed to talk to him about it. I dreamed that my baby had died and I was holding her and screaming and crying, "My baby! . . . . My baby! . . . My baby is dead!"

The dream shook me up so bad that I earnestly prayed with Kyle that the dream would not be fulfilled and God would not take my baby away from me. I hope he heard my prayers. I did take this dream to be a warning and tried to be extra careful with my children.

Sunday, January 28, 1979.

It's been a while since I last talked to you. Ann got sick after I forgot to pick her up from school. I had dragged George and Merri Ly down the hill in my little red wagon and got there a little too late. She had already tried to find her way home. I looked all over for her worried sick for her. I called the Police to see if they found her. It was a cold snowy day, and my babies were getting very cold. Some people found her crying in a store and called the Police and they brought her home. I was so relieved; I was crying and thanking God my daughter Ann didn't die out in the cold.

I put her in a warm bath to warm her up. I made sure it wasn't very deep. She was so tired that she fell asleep in the bathtub. This frightened me. I didn't want to lose my daughter to drowning. Then I put Merri Ly and George in the tub to clean them. Merri Ly slipped and fell on the bath spigot and got a big knot on her head. This also frightened me. I didn't need this right after my horrible dream.

Ann was sick from wandering in the cold while she was lost. Kyle and a friend named Frank blessed her and almost immediately, she was well. The power of the priesthood was very strong. I thanked the Lord for healing Ann.

On Friday night, Kyle and I decided we hadn't had enough time together as a couple, so we wanted to go out on a date. We asked my grandmother if she could watch the children, and she said she could. My brother was staying with her and seemed to be doing quite nicely. We were going to see a British Comedy, which were very popular at the time. A comedy seemed to be in order after the terrible things that had been happening to my children. When we went to drop the children off, Merri Ly was clinging to me more than ever. "May I take Merri Ly with us?" I implored to Kyle. "She doesn't seem to want to let go of me and I wouldn't mind taking her with us."

"No," he replied. "She needs to learn to more self sufficient and not so dependent on you."

Peeling her little arms from around my waist, I gave her one last kiss, and gave a kiss to Ann and George and said, "Goodbye."

Merri Ly cried as I went out the door and I almost cried, too.

While at the movies, I got very bored with the British humor, and was concerned about my children and wanted to leave early. Kyle obliged and we went back to my grandma's house.

When we came back, I started counting the lumps in the beds. My grandmother thought she was doing my children a favor by putting all the children in her bedroom, including Merri Ly on her old brass bed. "One, . . . two . . . Where's the third lump?" Anxiously, I felt around for the light switch. I found the third lump, Merri Ly below me! She had twisted and crawled off the end of my Grandma's ill-fitting mattress and had fallen off the end of the bed into the clenches of the brass spoke and the bottom of the bed. Her neck was held tight by the cross bars while her body was on the other side of the vertical brass bar.

Desperately, I wrestled her out of the spoke crying and sobbing, "My baby! . . My baby! . . . My baby is dead!"

Immediately, I started administering CPR on her. It was like blowing into a little doll. I was so distraught, I was going into hysterics. Kyle took over the CPR and had me go call 911. Ann and George had awakened at this time and saw what had happened and started crying for their little sister. My hysteria had taken over so intensely, I was screaming and crying and couldn't think. Kyle had to yell the numbers 9-1-1 to me because I couldn't remember them. Then I couldn't remember the address to my Grandma's house. He had to yell to me what they were. All I could think about was my baby was dead! I was beyond thinking . . . I was in shock!

"Oh Lord," I cried over and over, "don't take my baby!"

I screamed and cried and my poor children were crying. I kept hugging my Grandma who was blaming herself for putting my baby on her bed. My brother was so upset and was running around telling me, "I told you not to leave your babies here. This house is too dangerous for babies."

The paramedics finally came. It seemed forever. Kyle said they tried to put a tube down her throat, but that didn't seem to be working. He told them to continue resuscitating her. They were kind of mad at him for telling them how to do their job, but they did it anyway. Then they started to ask us questions like it wasn't an accident that she fell over my grandmother's bed. They were trying to see if we ad actually killed our own baby on purpose. I was dumbfounded! I couldn't believe they would ask us that or even think something like that! "Why would I kill my own baby?" I thought while I was crying and in hysteria. "I love my babies so much that I couldn't imagine deliberately killing them."

Kyle explained to them what had happened and got a little angry with them about their remarks of how the baby died. He finally convinced them that it was an accident, and they seemed satisfied. Finally, we got to the hospital that they had her in. I waited in the lobby for about an hour before the medical staff came to us with the news that she was alive because her heart was so strong, but they would have to transfer her up to Primary Children's Hospital where they were more equipped to care for her.

We followed the ambulance as it sped toward the hospital, but we were stopped by a policeman for speeding. When Kyle explained that our daughter was in the ambulance, the cop didn't give us a ticket, but explained that we were not supposed to follow the ambulance so close. "You don't need to get killed yourselves," was his explanation. We slowed down and finally got to the Children's hospital.

We then went up to intensive care to see our daughter. She had so many tubes in her and they had to drill a hole in her skull to allow the fluid to drain off her brain because of the swelling. They then informed us that they did not know if she had any brain damage or not. "We'll have to find that out later," they stated. "Right now, we will have to stabilize her. She does have a strong heart. That's probably shy she is still alive."

Our little family quickly became one of the many "couch" families anxiously waiting in the lobby of the hospital. The medical staff understood our dilemma and didn't mind us staying there as long as we did.

When Merri Ly was stabilized, they performed some EEG's on her brain. The last scan was even worse that the first scan. She had some activity, but not enough to ever function normally. She was in a coma. No one knew if she would ever awake.

It hurts all of us to see our once beautiful, active baby and sister lying so stiff. Her eyes are like glass. She doesn't respond to pain. They have holes all over her little body for all different kinds of tests.

I didn't know what to pray. I thought of the baby that Kind Solomon had threatened to cut in half when the mothers couldn't agree which baby it was. I almost wished my baby had died than to be left in the non-responsive comatose state. I began to doubt God and modern medicine. Who had the power to heal?

Chapter 24

Questions

Tuesday, January 30, 1979.
Dear Journal,

My husband and I are beginning to get used to the idea that Merri Ly will not be with us long. It isn't any longer the initial shock that it was at the beginning.

Debbie came to see her 'little buddy' and had given her a blessing. I thought about her blessing about being able to save some of her loved ones that are close through the power of prayer. Merri Ly was very close to Debbie. Debbie would always pick Merri Ly up and say, "Hi, Buddy! You're my little buddy, aren't you?" while she would tickle Merri Ly under her chin and belly.

Debbie would swing Merri Ly around and she would laugh and giggle with delight. They got along so well.

My Mom came up from California to watch George and Ann. My Dad later came up with my sisters Suzanne and Darleen. I have seen in my lifetime many miracles wrought by the great faith in the Lord that my Dad had. Between him and Debbie, I felt I had a pretty good team.

Debbie stated she would fast and pray and was able to come up on Wednesday night and Thursday. She stated she would pray and present her blessing to the Lord and say, "See this promise? I'm doing my part, now you keep your side of the bargain."

It was so comforting to have such a wonderful friend in Debbie. She had so much faith in God.

There was another little boy in the hospital that just got out of heart surgery yesterday. He seemed to be doing quite well. His parents were happy about the outcome, but this morning, I found out that he died. I asked one of the other "couch" family mothers what had happened. She said, "All at once, all of the beepers went off. They shooed everyone out of the room and the little boy died. They couldn't figure out why, so they are doing an autopsy on him now."

We became a "couch family." We ate, slept, and camped out at the hospital. It wasn't a great life, but when your loved one is at the hospital, you find yourself wanting to be as near to your baby or child as you can. At least they have very nice couches at this hospital. The nurses and doctors are very sympathetic, but also very busy. I didn't realize how complicated ICU really was until I was personally involved.

Wednesday, January 31, 1979.

Well, today is another day. Merri Ly is still in ICU (Intensive Care Unit) and still not reacting to light or any stimulus. Her eye pupils are getting smaller, which the doctors can't seem to explain. Also, they enlarge when you put light in them. Kyle suggested that we massage her feet for stimulus. We do that plus touch and rub the rest of her body. Some days, her arms are tense; some days her arms are flaccid, which are just some more very strange things about her.

Debbie couldn't come to pray for Merri Ly. I think it was something about a snow storm and no transportation. This made me sad that I couldn't see my friend and not be able to cry on her shoulder about her 'little buddy'.

I still don't understand why Merri Ly is still clinging to life.

Frank and Charles were some men that Kyle had been talking to about polygamy. They volunteered to pray for her. They gave her a blessing that she would stay long enough to fulfill her mission here on this earth.

Kyle and I had many questions concerning Doctrine and Covenants 132 about Joseph Smith taught about Plural Marriage. It appeared that the Lord not only sanctioned it throughout his Holy Bible with his Holy Prophets Abraham, Isaac, Jacob, Moses and others and the law never changed in the New Testament and the Jewish law had never changed, even to this day. When God commanded Joseph Smith to practice this ancient law, he initially refused, until God sent a Holy Angel with a sword and commanded that he practiced the same law that his ancient Prophets practiced.

I always knew all my life that Joseph Smith was and is a true Prophet of God, called by God in these Latter Days to restore the true Gospel of Jesus Christ. I started to feel that the Church had done a great disservice to Joseph Smith when they rejected the law of polygamy given to Joseph Smith. After all, my earlier ancestors in the Church were polygamist.

When Kyle found out about these men and how they felt about all the laws laid out in the Doctrine and Covenants , he became interested. These men seemed to be stalwart men of God and spoke the truth of the Doctrine. They also taught about the Order of Enoch or the United Order which Joseph Smith taught the early Saints. The Church has since abandoned this principal, also. There were many other things that they brought out that Joseph Smith had taught and was commanded by the Lord for the Church to follow, but the modern Mormon Church had abandoned many of them. This became troubling to me and I was going through a very difficult time of my life. The more I found out, the more troubled in the spirit I became.

I believed in the Church and was raised in it all my life and felt it was true. But, below the surface, there were many things that I was finding out about how the present Church had abandoned many of Joseph Smith's original teachings.

The more Kyle and I searched the scriptures, the more disappointed we were in what we found. We decided that we would like to go back to original practices, practiced by the Church. We were going by God's commandments, "If ye love me, keep my commandments."

Chapter 25

Sustaining Her Body

Sunday, February 4th, 1979.
Dear Journal,

Kyle and I saw the bishop of our Ward. He was a magnificent, sympathetic man. He told us that he would take care of the bills at the hospital. I do love this Church that I grew up in. I don't ever want to be excommunicated from it if I can help it. That would mean the end of being able to go to temple if I was.

Kyle and I went to another meeting today. These people are the followers of a man called Rulen T. Jeffs. This group of people are striving to carry on the principles of polygamy as received from John Taylor, a former Prophet of the Church. They claimed that John Taylor stated before he died, could foresee that the church as a whole, would reject the principle of polygamy, so he set apart and gave the keys of the Priesthood and ordination of Celestial Marriage to a small group of men to carry on the practice of polygamy so that, "Not a year goes by without a baby being born in a Celestial Marriage of plural marriage."

These people seem to a very righteous people. Their leaders are fire and brimstone speakers which is really good to hear. None of them had made previous notes to read from like the Mormon Church had. They all spoke from the Spirit of the Holy Ghost which I felt very strongly. They all wore white ties. I had never seen so many men wear white ties before.

The women were also very beautiful. They never cut their hair and had it done beautifully in buns on top of their heads. My husband and I were disappointed about the lack of beards. This is probably because Kyle loved growing his beard. He had it a lot like Brigham Young wore his.

I was so moved by the spirit of that meeting, that afterwards I wanted to shake hands with him. I was scared to look into their eyes because I felt like I was a sinner. I burst into tears and wanted to get out of there. I felt like the woman who wept at Jesus' feet and cleaned them with her tears and dried them with her hair.

We had left the children with Irene, one of the sweet women in this group. We came back from the meeting and stated that we needed to go to the hospital to see Merri Ly. She agreed to look after the children.

When we arrive and looked in on Merri Ly, she was doing the same as before. ICU nurses couldn't find any more surface veins for her IV's and so they would have to cut down to get to the veins. She would have cuts and stitches all over her body. Of course, this was depressing news.

Monday, February 5th.

This morning, when we called the hospital, the ICU nurse stated that Merri Ly had broken out in a rash. They think she may have developed an allergic reaction to the antibiotics they were giving her.

It is so painful to see my beautiful baby girl to have to go through all this misery just to keep her alive. Is modern medicine so wonderful as to keep someone alive past their life? I have to ask these questions sometimes just to keep a check on reality.

It's so disheartening to see her just lying there, between life and death, when she was such an active baby before this horrible accident. Kyle said he would like to continue working with her for another week or so – he doesn't want to give his baby daughter up, yet. Neither do I.

My mother stated that he wouldn't give up on Ann when we had to fight for her, so why would he give up on a child that is his? She also said, "What are you going to do? Just keep on sustaining her body and keep on bringing different people in to try to heal her?"

This statement from my mother really hurt. It hurts me now more than ever because I am finding myself doing exactly what she said.

I really don't know what to do. I keep hoping and praying that this nightmare will go away and everything will be all right. Kyle, Debbie, and Alma keep reassuring me of this. I'm beginning to question everything in this world. Why . . . Why . . . ! did this have to happen to me. Did I do something to deserve this trajedy?

I keep on asking the Lord, "What is going to happen? What shall I do?" I felt so much like Job in the bible when he was going through all of his troubles.

"I must go on, I have other children to take care of," I finally concluded. "They need me, too. I must start to care for them and love them. They are going through the same hardship I am going through. We must be together in love and understanding."

We are trying to get another car so I can have some transportation to get to the hospital while Kyle goes to work. Our blue Cortina blew up. I must get work around the house, so until later.

Sunday, February 11, 1979.
Dear Journal,

Yesterday was Merri Ly's 11 month birthday. The doctors have taken the screw out of her head since Friday. They took her off the manitol, Thursday. They took her off the respirator on Saturday, the they put a little tube down her throat to keep her from swallowing her tongue. She is eating so well through a tube down her nose that they are thinking of pulling her last IV out. They also pulled the bladder hose out. She doesn't swallow her spit, so they have to suction it out through the trachea hole in her neck. She looks a lot better without all of her tubes. Pretty soon, she may not need any except for her feeding tube that goes down her nose and the hole in her trachea.

She is moving every so often and stretches her whole body and reacts to different stimuli such as cold wash cloths. The doctors can't understand why her eyes fluctuate so much. They go from big to small quite frequently. They also can't explain why she is even moving. Everyday is a big improvement. Her brain waves look worse to the doctors in some ways, but when Kyle and I looked, we thought we found some very organized brain waves. But, of course, we are not experts in this field. We were just hoping and somehow grasping at every little straw we could find.

We had some other great Priesthood holders give her a blessing. They stated that we should accept whatever the Lord does. Also, they asked for her to have her back whole or take her to the Lord.

Kyle and I wondered if were being tested like Abraham when God told him to sacrifice Isaac, his only son. Or like Job when all of his family was wiped away in a whirlwind. Yet, they did not curse God and die. I pray to have that strength and faith in the Lord.

I talked to Alma on the phone yesterday because I needed someone to talk to. I was getting so depressed about what was happening in my life. She told me that she had a similar experience with her daughter Gloria. She said that Gloria almost died when she was born and almost died again when she was two months old from a disease that had killed 600 other babies in her city. She said Gloria was almost dead and she didn't know what to do. So she dedicated Gloria to the Lord. The next day, Gloria began to get better and proceeded to get well. The doctors were amazed and then told Alma she would probably be retarded when she reached seven years old. Gloria has been Alma's most brilliant child. She is intelligent beyond her years and has dreams and prophecies even more than Alma herself.

Alma suggested that we should dedicate Merri Ly to the Lord. Kyle thought it would be a good idea, so we are dedicating Merri Ly to the Lord.

The nurses are now beginning to show us how to care of Merri Ly so we can take her home. This could be a problem, because as of right now, we have no home to take her. Miracles can and do happen, however. Kyle recently got a very good job in a new company that designs aircraft flight simulators and he is now one of their programmers. We also found a home on Ninth East, not too far from the hospital, in case an emergency happens with Merri Ly.

One of the nurses is named Connie. She is really good to us. There is another nurse named Stephanie, whom Kyle and I know we have seen somewhere before, but we just can't figure out where. She looks so familiar. She probably thinks we're strange because I keep on bringing up different places where I might have seen her. They have all been wrong. I probably was good friends with her in the previous life.

There is a lady at the hospital with her child from the Southern Polygamist's group of Short Creek under the Allredite group. She's also somehow connected with group we have gone to in Salt Lake City. Her daughter is in semi-ICU with tubes in her lungs because of pneumonia. The lady seemed very nice and had her hair down one day as I was passing by. It was trailing several feet on the floor. I had never seen such long hair before in my life. This group she was associated with was the same group that was connected to the Doctor I had stopped going to when I found out he was a polygamist.

It is such a small world.

Kyle wants me to think about joining these people, but I just don't know about it. My mind has been in such a quandary about everything that has happened to us and our children, it makes me want to wait a while. I believe that I should practice all the laws of the Lord, even polygamy if the Lord told me to do it, especially if I am to obtain the highest degree of glory as stated in the Doctrine and Covenants. I just don't feel right about leaving my precious beliefs and teachings that I had been taught all my life and I certainly don't want to be ostracized by my beloved Church.

I pray that the spirit of the Lord will guide me to do the right things concerning these matters.

Kyle wrote a poem in my journal today. It goes as follows:
Somewhere lurks a thought or two
Innocent and curious.
Somehow there's a promise or two,
Solemn and wise.
Someone visits a time or two,
Reluctant and shy.
Sometime in a week or two,
She'll return and stay.

Smiles, frowns and lives all upside down,
Slow and determined, but ever anxious;
Coming again and again to the same closed door;
Refusing to be caught, having done less than all we could.
Soon, it'll be your turn, God.
Then we'll wait no longer,
And the hunger for her presence
Will exist in dimming memory only.
Might you like to come and stay with us,
'Ere you leave this world in finality;
Rotten in some respects it is, we admit.
Real and beautiful, too.
Ignorance you'll lose and innocence, too.
Life's worth living with it's living and learning.
You might even regain your innocence if you'll try.
Lift an arm, open an eye, think the thought,
And soon you'll know nothing' missing here to make us and you happy
Except you. Kyle

Chapter 26

Coming Home

Saturday, March 10, 1979.
Dear Journal,

It's been a little while since I last wrote to you, but I feel I have a good reason. This has been the first time I have been able to set down for en minutes at any one time, and that's only because I am staying with Merri Ly all day to learn how to take care of her when we take her to our house. Yes, I did say house . . .You heard right. We are going to be able to take her home Monday or Tuesday of next week! We are so excited! No more "couch family" for us! We actually get to live at our own little home while we are taking care of her! I know this seems strange to get excited about all of this, but it has been so tiring to have to go the hospital to visit and care for my baby every single day.

Kyle will be staying with her on Sunday (tomorrow) all day so he will be able to learn to take care of her, also.

Today is also Merri Ly's birthday. She is turning one. I don't think we are going to be able to celebrate with a cake, but we'll arrange something. I sang Happy Birhday! to her and she seemed to smile at me when I gave her a big hug. I talked with her and told her how wonderful she was to me and her Daddy and George and Ann. I gave her the range of motion she needed, suctioned her lungs and washed her hair and gave a sponge bath, just as the nurse instructed me. Caring for someone that was a complete invalid was all new to me. I wouldn't have dreamed in all my life I would have to do this for anyone, especially my baby.

So, about the house, after looking for two to three days for a house after the hospital informed us we were going to take her home for us to care for her, (we knew we couldn't take her back to our little one bedroom apartment) we found a house not to far from the hospital. Believe me, I was going stark raving mad, yelling at Kyle and Kyle yelling at me for no good reason, except the amazing amount of pressure we were both under to get a house within the week that would accommodate Merri Ly's suction machine and mister machine and Ann and George and Merri Ly's bed and a place for Kyle and myself to sleep and call a home for our little family and still be within a price range that we could afford . . . .whew! It makes me tired just writing about it!

We finally found one on Ninth East, it wasn't too far from the hospital in case something happened and we needed to rush Merri Ly to the hospital. It was for $37,000, which wasn't too bad. Prices were going so sky high that we felt that was a good price. It was newly remodeled, newly painted and carpeted, new kitchen, new wallpaper, nice shelf basement in which we could put both of her motors in and not have to listen to them while we were sleeping. It was a brick home with a fireplace. It had a matchbox front yard with a gigantic tree and a nice front porch, shared driveway with the neighbors, a garage in back that wasn't ours and a tiny backyard. It also had three bedrooms, if you could call the back little room a bedroom.

It's a nice older home that I won't have to do very much to move into it. I know I am going to enjoy it better than living in a one bedroom apartment. Kyle and I have been working hard to get everything out of storage in Provo. We still have a piano to bring up along with other furniture we had in storage.

We have been working around the clock to trying to get everything ready to bring her home and move our little family in to a comfortable home. As it looks now, it doesn't look like we will be able to.

We started to move in around March 1st or 2nd. Everything is such a big blur that I can't remember the days anymore. We were able to get some nice furniture from a trade club that Kyle belongs to. We got them from a lady named Summer. Her mother had just died and she had inherited a lot of furniture she didn't really care for. I didn't care, one man's junk is another man's treasure. I had to learn that the hard way. We got a big wood table with tree chairs, two bar stools, two nice stuffed chairs, and an expandable stool or bench and some lamps for about $700.

Kyle's boss had an old pink stove and fridge that he loaned or let us have. I was happy with the gift, but I ended up cleaning out the fridge before coming to the hospital today.

Talk about hectic! Kyle helped when he came home from work and I was working everyday trying to get the house ready.

Thursday, March 15th, 1979.
Dear Journal,

Well, we were able to get everything pretty much squared away before we brought Merri Ly home. The house is in pretty good shape. There are still things to do, however.

I had to quickly run down to Sears and get her a car seat carrier to take her home in. I brought her home around 12:30 p.m. The nurse that helped me was named Robin. She helped me load the baby and everything that came with her in the car.

Kyle had put the switch for the two motors on the crib. The crib was stationed in the dining room area situated between the front room and the kitchen. It was also near the bathroom and the bedrooms, so it was very centrally located. This was planned so she could be right in the center of everything. I could keep my eye on her while cooking, and George and Ann would be able to play with her and talk to her at any time.

Merri Ly had a little water bed to sleep on and we had gone and purchased more fake sheepskin a couple of days ago in addition to the one the hospital had given us.

Kyle and I worked out a system that I would take the day shift and he would take the nights. I don't know how he did it while working a fulltime job, but somehow we both worked together and pulled all of our efforts to do what need to be done.

She has to be fed every three hours by inserting a tube through her nose down to her belly, which we had to check to make sure it wasn't in her lungs. She has to be suctioned periodically when we hear her lungs start getting full of phlegm. She needs to be exercised with a full range of motion so her muscles won't contract. Equipment has to be washed with Joy daily, because Joy is the only detergent soap that rinses clean. She has to be bathed daily, changed frequently, and bed clothing changed frequently. It is extremely detailed care. It is all we can do to keep up with her and caring for our other children. I was so glad to have the motors in the basement. It would have driven us crazy to have to hear them 24/7.

Friday, March 16th, 1979.

I called Dr. Thompson, the Neurologist, at Primary Children's to see how her last EEG was before we took her home. He said it was very good! In fact, she is just below waking level and told us we should be expecting some more movement from her!

This was exciting news! Kyle and I were very excited about this news. We had noticed that she was opening her eyes and subconsciously looking at us which we felt was truly a miracle from the Lord! Thank you, Lord!

We were invited to go swimming with my sister Judy and her family. I inadvertently told her about the polygamist group that we were looking into. I guess I wanted to talk to someone about it besides my husband. She literally became ballistic!

"How dare you have anything to do with polygamists!" she screamed. "Get out of here! I don't want to talk to you any more! The Church is going to excommunicate you! You're going to Hell! Don't ever come back here if you are going to have anything to do with those people!"

What did I expect? With all brainwashing that we had been subjected to all of our lives being raised in the Church, it had taken a lot of convincing over the years for me to be turned by Kyle, before I was able to even consider or stomach the remotest possibility of even been seen or consider the polygamist way. As far as this little group is concerned, called the Jeffs, we will be joining them and getting baptized next Saturday. I now feel that if I am going to reach the highest degree of the Celestial Kingdom according to the 132nd section of the D&C, I would have to take this step. We all feel that we are Mormons, whether practicing polygamy or not.

Saturday, March 17th, 1979.

Kyle and I went to get baptized today and resealed and received the Holy Ghost by the Jeffs group. I felt like my sins were washed away and felt a great spiritual high. Kyle was feeling pretty good, also.

Chapter 27

Short Creek

Friday, April 13th, 1979.
Dear Journal,

Today, Ann and I had fun making molasses taffy. We love each other very much and have great fun together.

I didn't get started doing the Easter dresses as I had planned for her and I, but that was my fault. I have been feeling sick again with strep throat because I stopped taking my penicillin to soon.

Frank O., the polygamist friend of Kyle, brought over some Brigham Tea that he had picked in the Utah desert. He proceeded to tell me a story of his daughter having little red bumps after a bad streptococcus infection and how the tea had cured it completely within a week which was better than the penicillin he took. Others have claimed that it purifies the blood and make the body more able to get rid of diseases.

We had decided, that now we are bonafide polygamist, we needed to go down to Short Creek and check out the Church we had just joined. We went, we checked, we analyzed, and then we talked.

"You know, that all I care about is you and this marriage," Kyle stated. "Nothing else matters."

"Those are my sentiments, exactly," I replied. "We have gone through a lot, more than most couple have in a lifetime of a marriage in a very short time."

"So what did you think about our visit?" I inquired.

"I have always tried to be very honest and up front in my dealings with people, and you and I have worked on a very honest relationship in this marriage, but I find these people are very subversive, dishonest, and untrusting.

I just don't feel comfortable around them. They sure weren't friendly with us, either."

"I made the mistake of asking how many children were there in their family," I said. "They looked at me like I had asked them if they were from Mars."

"When God gave me that little dream to ask Frank O's daughter if she would like to come into our family, I thought the whole community would come apart," I stated. "How dare I have a revelation from God in a dream, and how dare I not go through the Elders. Doesn't anyone have free agency there? That was one of Joseph Smith's most important teaching was free agency. Without it, we are nothing in the Lord. No man can be forced into heaven. We all have to choose whom we will follow, Jesus or Satan. Those are the choices we have in our life. No one can do this for us but ourselves."

"I could see that there were the "rich" families and "poor" families in the community," stated Kyle. "There was no "equal" sharing in the community like they said they practiced. "I also noticed that there was a great inequality of the amount of wives that were distributed throughout the male population. Those that had the greatest "power" amongst them in the "priesthood" had the most wives, no matter how old they were and they seemed to have the youngest wives."

"They have envyings and strifes amongst them and I really don't feel any spirit of God with them at all," I interjected. "I do hope the Mormon church will soon see the error of their ways and go back to the old teachings of Joseph Smith."

"So, what do you want to do about our findings?" implored Kyle.

"I don't know, Kyle," I answered, "let's just lie low for a while, attend the Mormon church and just take care of things with our little family for now."

Driving home from Short Creek was a release of a lot of pent up emotions. It was nice driving back home through the Utah desert with all the shrubs, the red cliffs, the occasional grove of pines that sweetened the air with a sharp twinge.

"Stop the car!" I suddenly shouted. "I see a bunch of Brigham Tea bushes!" Indeed, there were a lot of the stick bushes, for they have no leaves on them. Kyle stopped while I got out and picked a whole bag full of them. I definitely picked a few years supply to take home. This made me happy after such a disappointing trip to Short Creek.

We talked some more about our relationship and our family as we made the long trip home to our children and our little home.

Merri Ly is reacting a lot more. There are subtle changes every day that are hardly noticeable except to us. Maybe we are look for more things than are really there. We are so hoping for a major miracle to happen and have to be happy for even the smallest little changes in our daughter.

George is with Grandpa and 'Cita' for a three week visit with them. I really miss the little soul around the house. I pray that nothing will happen to him while he is visiting them.

The house is coming right along. We may be able to close the deal of buying it in another week or two. We had to have it inspected and the inspector gave us quite a list that we have to complete before the deal can be closed. They are as follows: 1. We have to get screen doors, 2. guard rails for the steps, 3. repair termite damage in the basement by replacing some of the beams, 4. put screens on the windows, 5. repair the chimney stack and replace the loose bricks on the top of the stack, 6. straightening the roof line, plus a few other minor things.

On the south window, we are putting a planter in. It will expand the window out a little.

The reverberations of me telling my sister Judi about my associations with the Polygamists came home to roost. Her husband has now forbade her to have any more dealings with the likes of us. She told me that I had been brainwashed by my husband. I kind of had to agree with her on this respect, but I felt I still had my free agency on the choices I had made.

Oh well, I love her along with all my family. I just hope and pray they don't completely reject me for my beliefs. The Lord has stated, that unless you are willing to leave family and friends and all that you own behind and follow him, you are not his.

(paraphrased)

Well, it's getting late and I really must go now. Hope to see you again, soon.

Chapter 28

Change for the Worse

May & June 1979,
Dear Journal,

So much has happened in the last months. While I was taking Ann to the airport for her visit to her Daddy in California, she asked me a perplexing question, "Mommy, when am I going to be old enough to say I don't want to go to see my Daddy or be there for such a long time?"

I didn't know quite what to say, so I answered, "Honey, I don't know what to tell you about what your asking. When you get older, maybe we can tell the court you don't want to stay such a long time. Maybe they will change the times. But right now, don't hold your breath."

She seemed to be somewhat happy with the answer, but it made me sad that she had to go through with her lot in life. It is asking a lot of a child to have to be shared by divorced parents and carted back and forth between them. Never in my life did I think I would be divorced, but once again, I chose my path, and now my child has to pay for my choice.

We kissed and hugged, and waved continuous goodbyes until the plane was out of sight. I love her so much. It hurts to see her sad and have to go for so long. She is such a good helper to me around the house and great company with Merri Ly and me. She will soon be seven years old on the fifteenth of July. She has the maturity of an adult, almost, because of the things that have happened in her life. It is so sad to see a child that can't be a child because of the circumstances in her life.

George caught the chicken pox about four weeks ago from Francie's son, Jacob. Jacob is George's best friend and visits him a lot. I've already had them when I was a kid, so I didn't get them. But, Ann had caught them from George before she left and didn't know it, and she called and said she had them the same Sunday George had them. Vince even told me she had them in her ears and then gave them to her little sister, Michele. Kyle had never had them before as a kid, so he caught them, too. I had never seen an adult have the chicken pox and I would highly recommend that if you are going to get them, get them as a child.

I had never seen a person in so much misery as him. He had them everywhere including his eyelids! He had large sized boils all over his body and took a lot longer to heal than George did. Needless to say, he had to miss a few days of work until he got better and his boils dried. I likened him to Job when he got boils all over his body.

My Mom called and told me that a dear old friend of hers and the family's named Frieda Christenson, was dying of cancer. This greatly saddened me. I dearly loved Frieda. She was such a master story teller and I remember on the Halloween Parties that we had at the Church in Porterville, she would tell us the scariest stories, and then scream her wildest screams you ever heard, and scare us nearly to death and then would laugh the wildest laugh you ever imagined. We loved her. She was almost like our second mother. My mother and her would trade funny stories of their children together for hours on end. I grew up with them. Some of them even came out and worked on our farm. In fact, one of them wanted to marry me, but I was too enthralled with the tall, dark and handsome Yugoslavian, that I didn't think was a brother I had grown up with, so I didn't give him the time of day. My grandmother Eggman, 'Mom-Judy' later told me that if I had married him instead of Vince, I would've still been married. I had to agree with her.

This was some very devastating news Mom had told me. It made me sad to have to see her die. I was hoping to see her before she died, but I knew that would be impossible with my own daughter being so ill at this time. "Mom," I said sadly, "tell Frieda I love her and will see her in the next life to come if I can't get there before she dies."

"Okay, I will tell her," she answered. "How is Merri Ly doing?"

"Not too well," I answered. "I'm a little worried she is going to catch the chicken pox that is going around. You should see Kyle. I have never seen anyone that has had it as bad as him! He literally has them everywhere! Now I know why you should catch them when you are small."

We talked for a while about Ann and her just leaving and other things. It was comforting to be able to talk to my mother. She was always a very wise woman and I needed to reach out to her at this time. I had been going through so much turmoil in my life.

I am currently babysitting for Leigh H. She is one of Kyle's old girlfriends and she is currently separating from her second husband and needed someone to watch her hyperactive son. She is a very friendly person and suffers from rheumatoid arthritis. She literally hurts in every bone of her body. It would be awful to be in that much pain. She is very slender with dark eyes and hair. Her and I have become good friends. She helps me with exercising Merri Ly.

George has become what Alma called 'cipe' again. It can't be because of the baby inside me because it isn't due for another five months. He's acting the same way he did just before Merri Ly was born. He is very lovey-dovey – wanting to be held, then cross and fussy. It made me wonder if Merri Ly is going to wake up in a little bit.

Merri Ly has done some strange things in the last few days. Tuesday, she had a temperature of 102 degrees. We thought she would get the chicken pox. We called our doctor and he told us to give her ¼ Tylenol every four hours. After giving ¾ of the Tylenol the way the doctor prescribed, her fever went down. Instead of getting chicken pox, her body totally relaxed like a limp noodle and the stuff out of her lungs had loosened. One of our friends that had worked in the army corps stated that she might be coming closer to consciousness. Her eyes have been closed all the time as though she's taking a long needed rest. Her hands and feet are showing some signs of small movement, which is also very encouraging. We will have to get help on her legs, though, which are pretty badly out of joint from lack of use.

Sunday, June 18th, 1979.
Dear Journal,

I had to rush Merri Ly to the hospital yesterday. Her temp. was 93.6 degrees. She was very blue and was barely breathing. The reason I noticed was because on Friday, she was starting to turn blue. I called the doctor and he said to take her temperature every four hours. About 3 p.m. Saturday, George was asleep, so I decided to do her Range of Motion while singing her favorite little tune, "Roll, Roll, Roll your boat gently down the stream, Merrily, Merrily, Merrily life is but a dream." I noticed she had turned extremely blue and wasn't breathing right. I took her temp and tried to get hold of the doctor, but couldn't reach him. So I got into the blue-bomb Cortina and put-putted up the hill to the hospital. Kyle was following behind me with our Mercury Cougar after I had called him. He grabbed Merri Ly and ran her into the hospital while I was still trying to secure the old bomb so it would not roll back down the hill.

When I finally made it to the emergency room, doctors were frantically fighting to bring her back to life. The X-rays showed that she had a real bad infection of pneumonia all through her lungs. Also, her sodium level for the electrolytes in her kidneys were dangerously low, so low that the doctor stated that he had never seen anybody so low in his whole history of practice. It was 104 count – normal is 134.

They gave her sodium. They also have her on a respirator because she had quit breathing on her own and also antibiotics to try to get rid of the pneumonia. She takes a vacation from breathing on her own while the respirator is on her, but she will breathe on her own while it is off. But, she doesn't quite get enough oxygen into her system and turns blue after a few minutes. She did have some temporary kidney failure due to the low sodium, but her kidneys are working fine now.

She seemed to be improving and she still responds as she usually did before she went limp. This is very encouraging.

I called Ann Saturday night. She is over her chicken pox and says that Michelle now has them. "I am taking swimming lessons and I am learning how to float on my back, Mommy!" She sounded like she was having such a wonderful time. I didn't want to spoil her fun with what was happening with Merri Ly.

"You sound like you are having a great time, my little sweetheart!" I said with as much enthusiasm as I could muster. "I hope your little sister gets well soon. May I speak with Helena, please?"

She handed the phone over to her Stepmom, Helena. I talked with her about what was happening with Merri Ly and cried bitter tears. I had to cry to someone and it happened to be her. She was sympathetic and asked if she should tell Ann about what was happening. "No, please let Ann enjoy her stay with you. She has already seen enough tragedy for such a young person. She needs to have some fun for a while. Thank you for all you are doing for her. Tell her I love her and miss her. I have to go now. Bye." I hung up. I felt drained.

Today, I went up to the hospital and washed Merri Ly's face, changed her bedding, change the ties to her trachea, suctioned her, and watched her for about 1 ½ hours. I have had very little sleep lately. It has been so disheartening to see her in this shape. It takes a toll on the soul and God knows what my soul has been going through.

Kyle went and saw her this morning and then took George for some man to son time to some friends' house to do some plumbing for them.

Chapter 29

Saying Goodbye

M onday, July 9th, 1979.
Dear Journal,
  I feel that I should write to you today. My heart and soul has cried so many tears, I feel that I am drained of all feelings, yet I still cry more tears. It looks like Merri Ly is going to leave us for good. Her stomach has stopped functioning, her breathing is erratic, she has to be put back on the respirator about every third day and she is responding less and less as the days turn into weeks.

  Alma relayed a dream to me recently. She said, "Carla, I had a dream and it was about Kyle. He was holding Merri Ly high above the angels reach that were trying to take her to heaven. He wouldn't allow them to take her to heaven. He wanted to keep her on this earth."

  This dream was a revelation that both Kyle and I had to release her back to God. It was important that both of us release her and say goodbye to her.

  Of course, I had my own difficulties on saying goodbye to my precious little daughter. I didn't want to go through the trauma of seeing her die a second time. I felt if I had to go through it again, there would be nothing left of me.

  Merri Ly is over her pneumonia and electrolyte imbalance and kidney failure, but, her little brain and body is giving out.

  Kyle ceremoniously prayed over and finally released her from all the previous blessings he had given her to stay alive and any other blessings she received. I could tell he was deeply hurt at what he had to do.

  I decided it is not fair for her to have to live this life like this. After all, she will be with her brothers that were with her in heaven and all of our extended family and the whole family of God. Who am I to mourn her death? It is I who has to continue living in this mortal life of sin and error and might not even make it back to see her when I die. I almost wish I could go in her place, but alas, I cannot. She is her own person and I am mine. I am so happy that I could have this precious soul from God for as long as I did. She was such a bright and beautiful soul and was so delightful to get acquainted with.

Do I still hope for a major miracle for her to completely get well again? Of course I do! I must learn to say, "Thy will, not mine, be done, O Lord!"

The doctors at the hospital, in all of their understanding of life and death, pulled Kyle and I into their little office and privately told us, "Life is for the living, and the way your daughter is, is not living. She is just subsisting. It is time to let her go."

Fully knowing they were right, we had to agree to pull the plug.

PULL THE PLUG! !!! May those in this world that have ever had to go through the 'choice' to become like God and have to 'pull the plug' on their loved one, they know the agony that they go through and the heartache of letting a loved one go. I know your pain. God knows your pain. He promises he will heal our hearts. God! Please heal mine!

Tonight, after crying on my mom's shoulder and her consoling me, George and I took our little wagon and bought too many groceries. We ended up having to bring a shopping cart home. George helped me by pulling the wagon while I pushed the cart. He was such a big helper. I promptly returned the cart to the store. He's almost three now and he seems to be enjoying the attention of having the attention of Kyle and I all to himself. With Merri Ly in the hospital and Ann at her father's, it seems strange to only have one child at home.

Kyle, George and I took a trip down to 'Cita' and Grandpa Keith's for the 4th of July celebration. We could perch on top of their house and look out on the Provo Valley and see the entire Valley's fireworks. It was totally awesome.

I went over to see Alma for a couple of hours. We shared our love of our children and she let me cry on her shoulders and hugged me and let me know she loved me. It was so comforting to me to have her friendship.

We then saw old family movies of Kyle and his family when he was as young as George is now. There is such a startling resemblance of Kyle and George, it is truly amazing. The nut fell very close to the tree. The only difference was that Kyle had fuller cheeks than George. We had Keith's famous Borscht soup and all kinds of goodies that they lovingly prepared for us. It is so very wonderful to be loved by my in-laws. It is such a change from my last marriage.

I called Ann. She sounded cheery and happy. I didn't want to dampen her happiness by the bad news of our decision of pulling the plug on her little sister. She didn't seem to have any complaints at this time, so I was happy that she was happy.

My mom just called me and told me about Dad having an accident on Sunday. He was at the San Francisco market selling his oranges and had just carried a box of oranges to a lady's car when he tripped over a parking lot concrete block that had a bolt sticking out and fell backwards on it punching a hole in his pelvic bone. Fortunately, it had not broken the skin, so there was no external bleeding. But, the pain of the fracture was severe enough to have him go to the hospital for a week. After a week, he was going nuts and had to get out of the hospital. When I talked to Mom, however, she said he was in so much pain, that he was going back into the hospital.

Well, I guess this is about all for now, so I'll be seeing you later.

Chapter 30

Running Away

Saturday, August 12th, 1979.
Dear Journal,

I'm here in Spokane visiting my sister Terri in the home she designed and built with her husband. I decided to run to the ends of the earth because I did not want to watch my daughter die again. I left Kyle to do all the funeral arrangements for her and ran.

My parents were going to Spokane, so I took the opportunity to escape. I told Merri Ly I loved her and it was okay for her to die. I released her emotionally and physically. I told her I loved her dearly and asked her to say Hi! to all the relatives and her brothers in heaven. I asked her for forgiveness for my not wanting to see her die, for I was afraid that I might just change my mind for the doctors to pull the plug if I stayed. I told her I would see her in the next life, and we would celebrate my coming to see her again. This good bye was very painful.

Ann, who had come back from California, also spent some time with her beloved little sister. I don't know how it affects an eight year old to have to tell their little sister good bye knowing that she is going to die. I had to explain to her what was happening to her little sister when she came back.

"Mommy," she cried, "It hurts to see Merri Ly have to go back to Heavenly Father. I love her so much!"

"I understand, Ann," I cried, "believe me, it hurts me, too."

We both held each other along with George and tried to console ourselves with the inevitable passing of our little daughter and sister.

When I asked Kyle if I could go with my mother and father with Ann and George, and the reason, he seemed to understand and agreed to call me when Merri Ly died so we could bury her as a family. We had arranged to bury her next to his older brother, Larry, in Koosherim, Utah.

I don't know how much Kyle was affected by the trauma of having his little daughter die, but I do know him and were fighting a lot more than normal and he was increasing his abuse to me. It was hard for both of us and the strain was tearing us apart. Kyle gave me his permission for me to go with my parents, full knowing that he had a rough mission to accomplish. He seemed to understand my feelings about my not wanting to watch our daughter die again.

What happened next was almost like the Biblical Jonah and the whale.

My Dad just had his Suburban engine overhauled and someone had failed to tighten the long bolt that held the carburetor onto the engine sufficiently enough to keep it from fall into the engine. The engine ground to a halt and we were stuck in a little border town called Wallace.

Dad spent all of Wednesday and Thursday trying to fix the engine. When he needed a part, he sent Suzie and me on bikes over a very rough terrain of a freeway that was in the process of being built. The ten speed bikes were made for boys and had the tiniest little seats. I was six months pregnant and was compelled to wear long dresses and long sleeves as ordered by the polygamist group that we were with. This was to hide the very long legged and long sleeved undergarments that they had made for Kyle and I to wear. These were very different and much more crude than the 'mainstream' Mormon church had us wear when we were married in the temple. At least we could wear shorts to our knees, pants, and dresses with capped sleeves and lower bodices.

Geez! I must've looked quite a sight! Fat and pregnant on a boys' ten speed bike, with a long dress with long sleeves. We had to ride five miles to the auto part store for a $0.50 cent part and back. I was not used to the skinny little seat for my oversized pregnant butt and was bruised in the crotch and painfully sore all over my body.

When my Dad with our help, finally did get the engine back together, with the help with some Mormon church member, we anxiously turned on our motor. To our dismay, the engine water quickly ran into the motor and mixed with the oil. This was not good!

Having no other alternative, we called Terri and she came and got us. On Thursday, I slept most of the day. I was so sore and exhausted from the trip. The rest of the family went to a little park in Spokane and Dad had to go to San Francisco where he had left his new diesel truck to come on the trip so he could haul the car piggy-back to Terra Bella.

On Friday, Aunt Dolores, my mother's sister and her husband Rudi, a doctor, took us to her house in St. John, Washington. Their house was a beautiful older home with fantastic woodwork throughout and she had a magnificent garden outside. She took us back to Terri's house around dark.

It was a lovely visit. This was the fist time that I had ever visited with this Aunt and Uncle. I hope it won't be the last.

On Saturday, Dad came back with the truck, so that evening, the car was loaded onto the truck and we headed to California riding in the Suburban on the back of the truck. It was kind of fun. There was enough room to sleep and take it easy. We didn't have to worry too much about going to the bathroom, for our family inherited our small bladders from my father, so we got to stop often enough to use the restroom.

On Sunday, we passed by magnificent Mount Shasta. The snow peaked mountain was so stately and beautiful. We didn't have time to explore it at this time. Maybe in the future I would come back.

On Monday, we finally ended our trek to Terra Bella to my parent's home. Very shortly upon arriving, Kyle phoned and informed me that Merri Ly had died. I cried and told Ann and George that we needed to go back to bury their sister. They cried when they heard.

My parents, being very pressed for money after all that had happened, could not go back to Utah to help bury Merri Ly, so I purchased Greyhound tickets for Ann, George, and myself to trek back to Salt Lake City. It was not a pleasant trip back. George had to sleep on the floor, Ann managed to sleep on the chair along with myself.

On Wednesday, we arrived, exhausted and broken-hearted in Salt Lake City. Kyle picked us up at the bus station and took us to our home. He had Merri Ly dressed in a beautiful red dress, white tights to hid all the holes that had to be poked in her while in the hospital, and a little wind up bell that played a beautiful little tune. He had purchased a little coffin made for a baby that she was almost too small for her, but it was so beautiful with all the satin in it. He had placed her and the coffin on the living room table because, "Even though she was dead, I don't feel like leaving her in the car all by herself."

It was good for the siblings to be able to see their little sister and say their final goodbyes. They loved their little sister and I knew they would miss her.

What happened next totally caught me be surprise.

Kyle screamed at me, "Carla, you don't appreciate me! I was here alone to do all the arrangements while you took off and left me! How do you think I felt!"

"I'm sorry, Kyle," I replied sadly, "I didn't want to watch her die again. I hope you will forgive me.

"No!" he screamed, "I cannot forgive you . . . you bitch!"

He then got a hoe handle, chased me onto the front lawn, knocked me down, and held the hoe handle to my throat and threatened to kill me, screaming, "You ungrateful bitch! You bitch! You Bitch!"

I was scared for my life and struggled to get him off me.

"Please, Kyle, the kids are traumatized enough to not have to watch you try to kill me!" I cried. "Let's try to work this out!"

Getting up off the lawn, with difficulty, and hoping he wouldn't try to attack me again, I went into the house and cried almost inconsolably. Ann and George were crying and scared, also.

The next day, after a fitful night's sleep, the traumatized little family made the trek down to Koosherim to bury their loved one. Keith and 'Cita' were able to come and help us bury her.

Merri Ly died the 15th of August, 1979.

Chapter 31
Concrete and New Birth

Benjamin Franklin L. was born, November 20, 1979. Weight: 8lbs. 7 ounces. What a beautiful, healthy boy! I counted all the fingers; all twelve of them, and the toes; all ten of them. Wait a minute . . . did I say twelve fingers?

"Where did these come from?" I asked Kyle, I mean I never saw six fingers on anyone before, so I was a little worried.

"I don't know where it came from," retorted Kyle. "I'll call my mom and see what she says about it, since you say it wasn't from your side of the family."

Kyle called his mother. "Mom, Benjamin has six fingers on each hand, is there anything in our family that might solve this?"

"You say your sister had fingers in her ears, and your aunt had six fingers on each hand? I never knew this before. How come I was never told before? he inquired.

He sat there a while and listened patiently while his mother made the explanation. Then he turned to me. "I guess you heard my side of the conversation and now know where the six fingers came from."

The birthing was so fast and furious. Francie, Patti (a college friend of Kyles' and Francies'), Kyle and I were peacefully playing cards in the beautiful new wing of Cottonwood Hospital in their Heritage II Birthing Center. You could invite friends and stay in the same room that you give birth in and the baby stays with you. I wouldn't have had it any other way. I did my research and this was a new trend in hospitals. Women didn't like to be treated like cold, hard baby deliverers the way the old hospitals treated them. Hospitals started seeing that women liked to have their babies at home, so you better have a home-like atmosphere if you are going to get them to have babies in their hospitals again. This certainly made me a customer. I also liked the bedside manner of the gynecologist that our insurance afforded us.

"I have to go to the bathroom," I suddenly said, and scurried my fat, pregnant body to the private toilet in my private birthing room.

As I was sitting there peeing, suddenly my water broke. "Oh, my gosh!" I yelled. Then I had a very sharp push. "I think I'm going to have this baby!"

Don't get me wrong, I had gentle pain all day long, and just took my time getting to the hospital. But this was serious. My body started to push and push hard. I waddled back to bed as fast as possible and said, "I think you better call the doctor, I think this baby is coming soon."

After getting the doctor to come in from a Youth night at the church, I had Benjamin three hours later from the first major push. It happened so fast! I was having Kyle hold my hands, Francie get ice for me, and Patty get fresh, cold cloths all at once. I never felt so rushed in my life!

When he came out, he was pink and had a healthy cry. He sucked all the colostrums on one side and waited a small while and then sucked all the colostrums from my other breast. Believe me, my breasts were huge! He then seemed somewhat contented and went to sleep in the little bassinet next to my bed which the hospital provided.

The pull apart bed that also served as a delivery table was reassembled and became the king size bed again, and Kyle and I were able to sleep together. Neat! Of course, Francie and Patty had gone home, so Kyle and I were alone.

"So, what do you want to do about the six fingers, Carla?" Kyle asked.

"Did you know that Ann Bolyn, King Henry's second wife, had six fingers?"

I said. "I don't know if he would like to go through life being different than everyone else. He might come back to me when he is older and ask me why I had the doctor cut them off and I would have to explain to him why I did."

"It's your decision, Carla. You do what you think is the best for him."

The next day, I asked the doctor to cut them off. He tied a string around them, and the fingers eventually fell off.

Ben was such cuddle baby. He allowed me to hold him and rock him as long as I wanted. It was such a comfort after losing Merri Ly. It was like he was helping me replace my ache and loss of his sister that he would never see on this earth.

He had such a huge appetite, that I found myself taking a huge glass of water to bed with me just to hydrate myself in the middle of the night. He was wearing twelve month clothes at three months and was growing so fast he is already starting to get up on all fours. He is turning, rolling over, and acts like he's going to crawl already!

George is doing very well as the older brother, except I have to have Ann interpret everything he says. At four years old, he seems to speak Martian. Ann and him seem to have the twin syndrome of a private language that nobody else can understand except themselves. He also seems to have a thing about ears. He keeps on putting his ear against my ear and substitutes the front of his words with a lot of H's.

I had a hearing specialist analyze his hearing. Apparently, on one side, he hears normally and the other ear is a little tighter, so he hears differently in that ear. I took him to the speech pathologist who worked with him for about six weeks, and he is talking so much better now. He loves to read to me and now I can understand what he is reading. This is three and a half now.

Ann has been sick the last couple of weeks with a cough which I hope she will get over soon. She is doing very well on her piano lessons and quite well in school. I have a little chart for her piano for six days. If she practices six days, she gets a surprise. Last week, she got a Barbie trunk. She put all her Barbie's in it. She was so happy. This week, I think I will get her a kite. We will go fly it at the school.

She is so pleased with this system that she makes sure she never misses a day.

I'm starting to feel like doing more now after three months of feeling a little tired after the birth of Benjamin. It really takes a lot out of you to have a baby. I'm taking exercise classes Tuesday and Thursday to attempt to get my blimpy figure back into shape. After having three kids in four years, it isn't easy to get my figure back. I'm also taking precautions not to have another baby so soon. I definitely found out that nursing babies did not stop me from having another one, as my cousins' wife claimed worked for her. I had to face the fact that I was a 'fertile Myrtle' and had to have precautions if I wanted a little space in between my babies.

In order to bring more money, I took in babysitting and selling lighted Frisbees. We'll see how this little venture does. I started to baby-sit a child George's age and another tiny baby. I decided that three babies were just too much and continued to baby-sit only fourteen hours a week. The extra $130 a month helps out in food and extras.

One day Kyle told me, "I'm going to move Scott into our basement. He needs a place to stay."

"I don't want Scott in our basement," I retorted, "he is the biggest slob I have ever seen! He only has a small path you can go on to get from one room to the other!"

"He needs a place to stay because he is getting kicked out of his apartment, besides he is an old college buddy of mine," Kyle yelled back. "Besides, it will only be for a month or two."

Reluctantly, after much yelling back and forth, I had to relent. I did not want a repeat of Kyle nearly killing me. The thought of Scott moving in with us sickened me. He was homosexual and he was also Jewish. Not that I had anything against either faction, I just felt he would be invading our little home.

No sooner did he move in, but he started some kind of concrete jungle in my postage stamp front yard.

"This pond will be for the tarantulas, and this little grotto will be for the poison lizards," he would proudly tell me.

He would sell his blood for eighteen dollars a week just so he could buy more concrete and cigarettes and beer for his weekly work on my yard.

"Do you realize what your buddy is doing in my front yard?" I yelled to Kyle. "I have had enough! I have little babies to care for. . .Our little babies, and your friend is planning to have poisonous vipers in our tiny front yard!"

"I want him gone! And I want the yard cleaned up and the concrete torn out and I want a lawn with some flowers in the front! Not some crazy man's dream of poisonous snakes and Black Widow spiders in our front yard! Get him out! I can't take it any more!" I screamed.

"He's gone on a camping trip," Kyle answered somewhat meekly. He was observing what his friend was doing, but didn't quite know how to politely tell him to stop. He then hired some help, tore up the yard, hauled it away, and brought back some sod, all in the same day.

When Scott came back, his clothes were packed, and Kyle took him to another friends' house to stay.

This wasn't the beginning of our marital problems. They just continued to get worse. Kyle was coming home drunk every night now. He started sleeping in the spare little bedroom in the back. He would scream at me continuously when he was home. I almost wished he had another place to go, the abuse got so bad.

As Benjamin got a little older, he was really crawling around extremely well. He was about eight months old and started exploring outside of the little matchbox yard. As I told you before, we lived on 9th East. Every week-day at four o'clock the streets had to be cleared, all the cars had to be parked off the sides of the street, and 9th East became a four lane highway. It seemed that no matter how Kyle and I put up fences and blocked the gates, Benjamin would find a way out of the yard to wander across the street to try to get to other side.

More than once, at the insistent yelling of George, "Mommy, Mommy, Ben is out of the fence and going across the street!"

Frantic with fear, I would have to fish out my baby boy out of the street while a wall of cars was barreling down upon us. I did not need to lose another baby, in this way or any way. I just buried one baby, I did not want to bury another!

I had had enough. I had to find a safer, quieter neighborhood and yard for Benjamin, one that didn't have a four o'clock highway next to my matchbox yard.

Chapter 32

Visions of Destruction

Sunday, March 29, 1981.
Dear Journal,

I was sick all day today. My left breast has an infection. I had a dream last night that Mt. Rainier was going to explode. I dreamed all the snow had melted from the mountain and it was beginning to let out steam. Kyle and I went to Seattle to warn his sister about the impending disaster of the imminent explosions, and left Seattle with his sister and her son. When we came back from Washington, Mt Rainier had not only blown its top, but all the surrounding volcanoes had exploded and completely destroyed the whole city and everything that surrounded it. Not only that, the earth shook so hard, a tsunami swept in and destroyed whatever the volcanoes didn't destroy. It was totally devastating. Everyone died.

I woke up in a cold sweat. It was so real, that it left me trembling. It was like I was right in the middle of the terrible scene, watching everything in vivid color.

This dream really bothered me, especially after the dream of my baby dying, and she actually did. I started believing my dreams. After all, doesn't God talk to many of his prophets in dreams?

Wednesday, April 22nd

I practically had the same dream as before about Mt. Rainier exploding. It was beginning to smoke. We talked with Kyle's two sisters living in Seattle to come on a two week vacation. We also saw Cindy, Kyle's first wife, and tried to talk her into coming to stay with us for a while. She wouldn't come. Then Mt. Rainier blew its top and all the surrounding volcanoes blew theirs.

The earthquakes and tidal waves and a new volcano practically devastated Seattle and all the surrounding areas. In the dream, Kyle went back to try to find Cindy. I don't know if he found her. My dream didn't go that far.

I told the dream to Kyle. "Kyle," I said, I have had this dream two times. It is such a bothersome dream. Why would I have the same dream two times?"

"I think the Lord is trying to warn you of impending disaster," he replied. "Do you think you can dream it again and ask the Lord what the warning signs are, so my loved ones can know what to look for? I need to know so I can warn them."

Not sure if the Lord would grant such a request, I did just that. That night, he showed me that the warning signal would be when Mt. Rainier begins to smoke, it is time to get out of Seattle and all the surrounding areas around it.

Post note: These dreams bothered me so much that later I did some research on the Mt. Rainier, Seattle area at Cal State Bakersfield while I was getting my Bachelors Degree. Apparently, the whole Seattle area is built right on top of a whole line of volcanoes. Mt Rainier is the most active of them and goes off about every 200 years and is due to go off at any time according to the time tables. I have also seen several shows on television showing the imminent destruction of the Seattle area from Mt. Rainier. It's pretty much how I saw it in my dream, only my dream is much more destructive.

I also was listening to Art Bell, a late night radio talk show host, and man got on and told how he saw the destruction of Seattle in a dream, only he saw it by reading the papers the next days after the devastating destruction happen. He saw in the papers that about 64,000 people had died from the devastating destruction.

I watched a Prophecy movie put out by Readers Digest. They were saying that people are starting to follow Psalms in the Bible for the countdown to the end of the world. Psalms 93 was for the year 1993 when floods covered the earth. Curious, I read ahead. In Psalms 104, it stated that "he touches the hills and they smoke . . . let the sinners be consumed out of the earth, and the wicked will be no more."

This scripture coincided with my dreams. I can no longer be silent about this. I warned my sister, Terri. She heeded my warning and moved to Arizona. She was living in Puyalup, right beneath Mt. Rainier. I hope others will listen, too.

We spent a very pleasant Easter at Kyle's parents' home. His oldest half-brother, David, was there with his wife and daughter. She and Ann had a very good time playing together. I like David and Donna, they are very good people. They treated me very nice, also. The weather was quite rainy that weekend.

On the way back home, Kyle and I had a big fight. We seem to be growing more distant from each other.

To spruce things up around the house so we can sell it, I have been painting the front porch, planting flowers, and cleaning the house from top to bottom. I hope we can sell it soon.

May 5th, 1981.

George went to 'Citas' for a week. When he came back, he said, "Mommy, I had a dream that Heavenly Father gave me the name of George Washington L. and then I went to God's Church with 'Cita'."

"That's wonderful, George, and your name is George Washington," I replied. "Are you happy with that wonderful name?"

"Yes," he replied in his utter honesty that only a child has.

Sunday, June 13th.

Dear Journal,

It's been a while since I wrote. I decided to take some time during church to write to you. Ann left for California June 1st to see her Dad. She had to miss a week's worth of schooling to do so, but the court demands that she see him, so she went.

I called her after she arrived in California and everything seems to be going good. I will leave her care in God's hands.

Suzi, our cat, had four kittens. Two of them died at birth and the other two have had to learn how to stay out of Benjamin's way. He's growing so big. He's eighteen months now and walking and running. If I thought he was handful when he was crawling, he is definitely a handful now.

George knows all of his ABC's. We have an ABC game he plays by the hour. It has words with pictures. He has already taught himself how to read. Since I took him to speech therapy he has never stopped talking.

George had another dream. He said he saw the world rolling up like a piece of paper or a scroll and he saw Jesus come and he kept the world from rolling up like the scroll and He kept everything from falling off the world.

"Mommy, I was scared, but Jesus made it all better," he said in frightened four year old voice.

I was beginning to wonder if my children were seeing visions just like I had seen. Then Kyle piped up and said, "He saw the very same dream that I saw when I was twelve or thirteen years old."

"It looks like dreams run in this family," I said. In a way, I was happy that my children were following in the prophetic footsteps of the prophets in the Old and New Testament and in the Book of Mormon. I was taught through these scriptures that anyone close to God could have these dreams and visions. Now, through my experiences and my loved ones, I could see this happening.

Chapter 33

Pat's Birth

February 27, 1982
Dear Journal,

This has been a very eventful time in my life. I had asked Kyle if I could have another baby, and of course he replied, "Yes, but it will be your responsibility when you have this baby."

"I'm willing to take the responsibility for this baby," I replied, knowing fully that my children would be mine even if all heaven and earth fell apart and even if I had no more help from him. I was just happy that he allowed my to have another baby at all, since my first husband wouldn't allow me to have another baby no matter how I begged.

Kyle is having a difficult time at work at this time and he has thought about quitting. I hope he doesn't. We need the insurance even though the plan we are in stinks. It is called FHP and it is the worst plan we have ever had. About three weeks ago, they discovered that I had a viral lesion on my vaginal area and told me it was herpes. I didn't even know what vaginal herpes was, let alone on how I got it.

"It is a venereal disease spread by sexual contact," they politely explained. "We are going to encourage you to have a cesarean so the baby won't come through the canal and either die or be blind."

I was furious! How did I get this dreaded disease? I didn't want to have to have my baby cesarean. I approached Kyle about it. "Why didn't you tell me you had herpes?" I demanded. "Is that why you always had that sore on your leg that came and went?"

"I'm sorry," he said. "I didn't think it would spread to you, so therefore, I didn't think I needed to tell you."

"So this is one of the diseases Francie was telling me about that she caught from you?" I was furious. "I thought you were going to be honest with me in this relationship, and now I have to go have a 'C' section because of what you withheld from me!"

I had to get over it, our relationship was getting ugly, and this was just one more problem I was dealing with. I had read in a Sunday paper that Israel had done studies on a possible help for herpes and found that Lysine, an amino acid, helped keep herpes under control. I promptly bought some and found that it helped my cold sores around my mouth and on the vaginal area. I was hoping I wouldn't have to have a 'C' section if it cleared, but FHP still insisted.

About this same time, George tumbled off one of our bar stools and broke his arm. I heard it break when he fell and knew it was broken. We rushed him to FHP. They took x-rays and told us they couldn't find anything broken. I insisted he broke his arm, but they said he hadn't.

After two weeks of him crying in pain every time someone touched him and not being able to sleep, I insisted on at least a partial cast, so he could have some relief. After two weeks passed, I noticed a bowing in his arm. I was so alarmed; I immediately took him to FHP again. This time, they found that he had broken his arm. They finally told us to go to a very qualified bone doctor.

We went, and the doctor put George in the hospital that night so he could re-break his arm the next day. Benjamin went home with 'Cita' and Grandpa. Ann stayed home with Kyle and I slept on the end of George's hospital bed that night.

In the meantime, Ann was coughing and not feeling well. She went to school the Friday George was getting his arm re-broken and I wasn't home to realize she was too sick to go to school.

I took her to FHP Saturday. That was a week ago. They just said she had sinusitis and sent her home with ampicillin. It didn't seem to get her well. She was coughing and having fever and chills and temps ranging from 100-102 degrees. Worried, I took her to another doctor at FHP. He also stated that he thought it was just a sinus infection and wanted me to change her medication to erythromycin.

She wasn't getting any better, and I was suspecting she had pneumonia, since I had it three times in my life and knew the symptoms. I was getting very angry with the incompetence of the doctors at FHP. I took her back to FHP two days later and had to have another doctor look at her. This time, I insisted that they at least take an X-ray of her lungs to see if there was something wrong. They finally did, and found that she had pneumonia. He told me to go ahead and use the erythromycin that was subscribed.

Kyle and I are beginning to get very fed up with the poor quality of this 'socialized' approach that FHP has. It seems that whats everybody's business is nobody's business and that seems to breed incompetence in everything that it touches, including doctors that seem to cover for each other. Kyle got mad enough to sue FHP for the expenses that were incurred on George's arm. They paid.

Benjamin is okay in spite of the hard fall he took on the slide across the street from 'Cita's' house at the school play yard.

Ann got better and is now able to go back to school.

George is taking the re-breaking of his arm in stride.

Kyle has been seriously sick and hasn't been able to come to the hospital while I was having Kyrt Patrick Henry L. (The Henry was dropped by the hospital.) He is such a beautiful baby of 8 pounds and 4 ounces. I fell in love with my anesthesiologist while going having the 'C' section. He blushed and apologized to Kyle, "I get that a lot, especially after giving them the good stuff."

Ann is at a friends' house named Dan and Cheryl. She's having the time of her life with them. They have lots of Guinea Pigs, snakes, and kids her age with lots of love which she badly needs at this time.

I am stuck here at this hospital trying to get my stomach to work so I can eat after my 'C' section. I snuck some bananas, some cheese, and some crackers and hid them under my covers so the nuns wouldn't see them. I hadn't eaten for three days while they were waiting to hear stomach sounds to see if my stomach was functioning normally. This is the pits. I do not want to have to go through another 'C' section again! Also, it is so painful, I can hardly walk, sit up or anything normal after the operation. I do not want to have to go through this again.

When Ann found out that I had another boy, she cried, "Mommy, I don't want to be a sister to three brothers!"

I'm very happy with Patrick. He's such a beautiful baby. He has long, dark eyelashes and dark eyebrows and blue eyes. He likes to nurse just like Ben did and they were both about the same weight when they were born.

Chapter 34

Tribulation and Escape

November 16, 1984.
Dear Journal,

It's been two years since I wrote to you. I'm too depressed to apologize. We did move to a much quieter neighborhood called Rose Park. The streets are quiet, with very little traffic on them. Our one/fourth acre lot has a very big yard with lots of trees on it. The house we live in must have been the original farm house in the area. It is at least 100 years or older. It is a white stucco house with a Mansard-style roof. The rooms inside are twelve feet high with rounded ceilings in the front room and main living room. It also has a rounded entry-way from those two rooms. The window casings have the most elaborate designs I have ever seen on any window. The whole house was made with a heavy lathe and plaster base which I found out later how hard it was to dismantle.

There are six doors leading into the kitchen, three bedrooms, one bathroom with a claw-foot metal tub, a back porch, and a large front, semi-enclosed porch that surrounds nearly half of the house.

George and Ben quickly put the huge yard to use. A friend of ours gave us a ride around crane that George rode and Ben constantly had to fix. There was definitely room enough to keep them occupied. When Pat got older, he went out to get acquainted with the dirt and the yard and played with his older brothers. Ann found friends in the neighborhood and played with her dolls. Kyle and I started working at remodeling the house in between our bitter fighting was getting increasingly worse.

We started first by closing three of the doors to the kitchen and made a central hallway. This gave the kitchen a more completed look. We then put a central heating and new cabinets and an island in the middle of the kitchen to modernize it. We then tore out the connected closets and put stairs up to spacious attic the house had. I textured the walls in the front rooms and dining room and painted them. Then I started tearing out the entire lathe and plaster in the two back bedrooms so we could lower the ceiling and have a livable upstairs. The upstairs was already four feet, so if we lowered the two main bedrooms four feet, then we would have a normal height large bedroom upstairs.

This was when I found out how much work lathe and plaster was to dismantle. It took two years of almost constant work with a crow-bar and a heavy mallet. I would shovel it out the back window into a wheelbarrow and then haul it to the every growing piles on the side of the road and back, continuously – day after day, month after month. The city hauled away most of it during the spring cleaning. I bet they loved my piles!

When the rooms finally were totally stripped, Joe, a professional mudder along with being the boiler operator at Blue Shield, and Kyle's old buddy came and helped me mud. He taught me a lot on how to make the walls look very good. We became very good friends. He was a very handsome Italian with a dark complexion, dark hair and dark eyes. He reminded me of my first husband, only a little shorter. He also had a very nice mannerism toward me, which was refreshing after the increasing verbal and physical abuse Kyle was doing.

At least these two rooms got done. We no longer needed to sleep in the living room. The boys got the side bedroom, and Kyle and I had the main bedroom, and Ann had the little bedroom the whole time that came off the kitchen. We were at least happy about the arrangements.

I became a Girl Scout Leader. As a leader, we planted gardens, painted the walls, taught crafts, sold cookies, and generally had a great time with the girls in my troop. Ann and the boys enjoyed these times and so did I.

Kyle was beginning to change the concept of what he called polygamy into what the dictionary meaning was; ergo – multiple contracts between individuals- not one man with many wives. That definition was polygyny. In other words, I could have just as many husbands as he had wives. We promised that if either of us found another person that we wanted to add to our little group, we would tell each other about them and include them. We were still going to the Johnsonite's polygamy group, which I found to much better than the Jeff's and the Allredites down in Colorado City/Short Creek. These people were much more honest and open about their relationships with each other.

We got acquainted with a man with three wives, two of them being sisters. These sisters had been main-stream Mormons going to BYU when they met their husband. They were quite disappointed about all the gays in the church, especially among the returned missionaries. They were quite thrilled to find a good man that believed in God and the basics of the Mormon Church and that was willing to have children. They didn't mind learning about polygamy and sharing their husband with his first wife who couldn't have children. Their arrangement was a loving, working, arrangement that I could see worked very well. They all worked very hard building their house from scratch. The women and husband worked at their separate jobs to support their growing family. I was truly awe inspired by their arrangement. I loved their honesty.

But, apparently, Kyle had grander schemes than this kind of arrangement. He started joining every strip club in Utah. He knew every one of the strippers and probably started sleeping with them. He would arrive at home blazing drunk on multiple pitchers of beer and tequila sunrises. Major drug and pot use became prevalent in his everyday use. He began putting time in fixing other women's roofs and houses while ours leaked. I helped him put on a roof of a 'friend' named Eileen, while I needed much in the way of repairs.

We never had enough money for food. My allotment for our four children was $25 every-other week. I had to start dumpster-diving at the local grocery store to help supplement our food.

While I was putting the finishing touches on the living room painting one day, the Lord spoke to me and said, "Kyle is sleeping with Eileen and has taken her for his other wife."

When I saw him, I told him what the Lord told me. He blew up and screamed at me with so much hatred that I had to take a walk just to get away from him.

To assuage his guilt of not telling me about his arrangement, he encouraged and helped me to move in a man named Alvin into our household. This man was in his sixties, an alcoholic and a smoker. And, he had only one tooth that was barely hanging on in the front. He also could never get his 'pencil dick' up because of his alcoholism. I don't know where Kyle met him.

Kyle and I then picked up a hitch-hiker named Tom and proceeded to move him in. He was younger than me by nine years and extremely handsome and well built with beautiful blue eyes and blond hair.

I moved both of the men to the uncompleted upstairs. Tom and I got acquainted slowly. He was very interesting with amazing stories and a very amazing last name. He told me stories about his family; his father was German and his family owned castles and large tracts of land in Germany. His mother was a Blackfoot Indian. He said they practiced a Satanic Cult of sacrificing. He also told me that he did time in Walla Walla, Washington State Prison.

I didn't know if he was lying to me or not. I had never heard of such stories in my life. It was kind of scary. But, at least he didn't yell at me, tear up my furniture, or hold a knife to my throat like Kyle was doing. He was leaving his family alone to fend for ourselves so he could eat, drink and be merry with his druggie buddies. I was hoping he would stay away. I couldn't stand him and I started to despise him.

I found that I had to go work and support my family. Kyle sure wasn't doing the job. I went to Kelly Temporary Services and started working part-time. Tom and I had temporary job together doing telemarketing for magazines. He was very good at it, but I wasn't. He was so handsome I found myself staring at him across the room. I found myself falling in love with this strange young man.

There were other men that a friend named Joan and I picked up at a bar. Their names were Don and Larry. Don and I ended up at my house, and Larry and Joan went to Don and Larry's apartment. I had never in my life picked up and brought anyone home and slept with them from a bar. This was definitely a first for me.

What a lover!

He sang to me, gently made love to me, sang to me some more, made hot love again, and was so gentle and caring. I hadn't had that gentle, caring love-making, in so long, it hurt. Then Kyle just happened to come home from one of his women-wives. This made for a very sticky situation. While we were in bed, I introduced Kyle to Don, and said, "We are in the middle of making love, could you please go somewhere else so Don and I can finish?"

Kyle complied, and we continued. This truly was awkward. But, this was the way our marriage was headed. I suppose Kyle was somewhat jealous of Don, because he took his .48 Ruger to show him what he had. I never saw Don again. I didn't think this was fair, because I never did this to any of his 'wives'. In fact, Eileen and I ended up working at the same company and talking about the same man, Kyle, at lunch. She started taking separate lunches from the group, and Kyle started really upping the ante on the abuse and wanting me to move out of my home into a little town called Wendover.

He then started telling me that Ann was old enough for him to 'break-in', and I told him if he touched her, I would kill him.

He promptly got rid of his gun collection.

Tom and I got close enough, (I still couldn't believe his stories) for me to decide to have a baby by him and to call him one of my husbands. I called up Kyle one day and said, "I'm going to have my last baby boy by Tom because I feel that you are not worthy any more to have a baby by me."

There was silence for a while and then he said, "Okay, if that's your decision, then so be it."

I set about making sure I did not get pregnant by Kyle. He seemed bent on polluting Tom by taking him to the bars and strip clubs. Of course, I went and got acquainted with all the beautiful women Kyle knew. I began to enjoy finding pleasure in the strip-tease of both men and women. They, the strippers, had their art down to a science. I also danced on the table tops at The Sun. This was a well known gay bar in Salt Lake City populated mostly by gay returned Mormon missionaries. I had a great time there.

Just to find out what it was like to get drunk, I arranged it with Kyle to take me to his Greek club. I drank everything on the wall and was a happy, blazing drunk. I found out what the 'Porcelain Throne' was and was taken home. The next day, my head hurt and felt like it was three sizes too big. All I felt like doing was moving a stack of wood from one side of the house to the other side, all day long. I decided I never, ever wanted that experience again.

I then wanted to find out what it was like to get high, so Kyle obliged me with a doobie. I only took one drag and found myself floating outside of my body with no control of my switches. This was such a scary experience that I thought, "If I'm not in control, who is?"

We were doing menege-a-tuas with Tom. Then Kyle found a young lady that we were doing this with. I told Kyle I didn't think this was right, but he didn't care. Of course, none of what we were doing was right.

I discovered I was pregnant, and Kyle started wanting me to move to Wendover. This was a dingy little border town with an ancient army base and wanting trailer parks on the Utah side of the border. There were big casinos and large, fancy homes and nice trailer parks on the Nevada side. He found a trailer on the Utah side for us. The town was one hundred fifty miles from Salt Lake City across the Great Salt Lake and the Great Salt Flats. I did not want to move from my home that I worked so hard on.

Tom left when I was four months pregnant, and I moved Alvin out to his brothers'. He had begun drinking continuously and had been sitting himself outside on the northeast corner of the house. He had since become so depressed that he quit the little job that he did have at a school, and was not taking care of his diabetes. I became concerned about him and felt that the poison environment that Kyle and I had made was no good for him or any one, even my children.

About this time, I started seeing the flames of hell around my feet. I didn't know what it was at first, but it didn't take long to figure it out. I stayed in bed day after day, month after month, so depressed and worried about my life and my children's life, that I felt like taking mine. Ann had to get the kids up, feed them, dress them, and get them to school. She was about twelve and a very responsible young lady.

I tried to escape my hell, and was having Satan appear to me. I wanted to escape out of this terrible situation and go live with my Mom and Dad. Kyle wouldn't let me. "I want to keep you here, because if you leave me, this arrangement that we have wouldn't look like it is working."

"It isn't working," I cried. "Our marriage is a mess, our poor kids are suffering, and I'm having the flames of hell follow me around twenty-four hours a day! I want to go see me Mom and Dad for a while. The kids and I need a break from this awful mess we are in!"

"I'll let you go on the condition you take Sheila with you!" he screamed. "That way, you will have to come back!"

I dreaded having to take the young lady, Sheila, with me. She was nothing less than a punk-slut. My Mom and Dad put up with her. I couldn't say anything and I was eight months pregnant. I made it back to the hell I was in – Kyle increased his abuse even more until I relented in moving out to the little ten x fifty foot mobile home to baby-sit for a living. Eileen had hollered enough about both of us working at the same place long enough for him to get rid of me to Wendover.

We had gone to check out the miniscule living arrangements when my water broke and I went into labor. It was a long haul back to Murray Hospital where I had arranged to have the baby. I stopped my labor pains on the way back and had lost all my water. The doctor and I decided to have another C-section and fix my umbilical hernia and get my tubes cut and tied. This would be my final baby.

John Quincy Adams came out a beautiful seven pound-thirteen ounce boy. This was the name he asked for in the vision I had when Merri Ly was born. I am a direct descendant of John Quincy Adams, the sixth president of the United States, and John was my sixth child. He was born on January 10th, 1985. I was given only one week to move out of my home by Kyle because his druggie friends wanted my home. I wanted to stay, but Kyle had increased his abuse so much and was tearing my furniture into splinters and also held a knife to my throat. I decided it would best for me and my children to get out of the terrible situation we were in. So, instead of enjoying my new baby, I was moving all my children and myself to Wendover in the middle of February.

Baby sitting was not an option there because everyone there was as poor as I was. Kyle did not provide enough money for us, so I had to look for a job in the Casinos. The pay was $4.00 per hour – three and half dollars less than I was making before as a secretary, but at least it was a job. It paid my rent, put food on the table, and I had enough money left over for Kyle to take and gamble with when he brought his friends out to harass me and gamble with. I was doing well! I was a money changer for the Mormons that would come out and gamble from Utah.

I knew I needed Jesus! I knew I needed to be saved! I had to get the flames of hell off me that surrounded my feet continually. I had never been taught in my church how to be saved in Jesus. We were taught that we had to do 'good works' all of our lives, then we would reach the highest degree of glory. I was never taught that there was a Hell, only three degrees of glory. This Hell that I was experiencing around my feet was so new to me, it was terrifying. I knew that if I died at this time, I would go to this Hell that was reaching out for me!

I had been a Mormon all my life, so I went back to Mormon Church to get saved. I found a Mormon Church in Wendover and I had my baby and my children in one hand and my tithing in the other. I went to the person I recognized as one of my bosses at the Casino and asked who I could pay my tithing to. He simply turned his back on us and walked away. All the other people in the congregation shunned us and walked away, also. They wanted no part of this raggedy family that looked like we needed help.

Stunned at the treatment they gave us, I said out loud, "It looks as if this Church doesn't need us. We will have to go somewhere else." I walked out with my children.

I proceeded to look at the other churches in the town and finally found a little church in the form of a square trailer on the old army base where the Japanese were interned during World War II. It was run by a 'lay' minister that worked at the school as a janitor and was attended by some very lost women with children that also needed Jesus. We prayed and sang and hugged each other and told each other our stories. We cried and hugged and sang some more. It was so informal and so wonderful. The children loved finding out about Jesus in the Sunday School class. I found Jesus! It was such a wonderful feeling. He took the heavy load off my shoulders and the flames away from my feet. I was not going to Hell anymore! What a blessed relief! I truly found that religions do not save you, only Jesus does.

In the meantime, I found a friend. Friends are very important in times of need. His name was J.D. He had just saved a woman from her pimp in Louisiana. His car had bullet holes to prove it. He was a cook at the restaurant on the Utah side and also had studied to be a Baptist minister. We became very close – and after making love one night, I poured out my soul to him. I had never told anyone what I had been going through with Kyle, and I cried and cried until I felt I had no more tears and then cried some more. He said, "Carla, any man that shares you with other men does not love you."

As honest as that statement was, I was so depressed and had no self esteem because of the mental abuse and torture that I had gone through for the past ten years that I could not believe it. I thought Kyle could still love me some how, even after all he had put me through.

Kyle came out and attempted to make friends with J.D. He even took J.D. back to Salt Lake City to get some supplies and clothing from my home there. J.D. and Kyle got into a fight after he told Kyle he could not love me if he shared me with other men.

Then, one day my mother just happened to come through Wendover on her way to take my sister, Darleen, to stay with her mother in Salt Lake City. J.D. happened to be there at that time. He proceeded to tell my mother all that had happened with Kyle and me, and told her, "If you don't take Carla and your grandchildren away from here and this situation, she will die."

"You need to load her and the kids in the car with whatever you can take with you and get them out of here," he reiterated.

My mother was so flabbergasted at what he told her, that she had a hard time picking up her jaw. I had never told her or anyone else what I had been going through. I was so ashamed of what I had done and what I had put my poor children through, that I wasn't about to tell anyone, especially my parents.

"I will take care of Kyle, don't worry about him," when both my mother and I were voicing concerns about him following us. Both of us were scared of him, because he had screamed at her before, also. He was a big, scary person.

The night before, Kyle had brought several of his druggie friends out to gamble, and then he brought one of them over to the tiny trailer in the wee hours of the morning. My bed was in the living room with all the boys in the larger back bedroom piled three high, Ann was in the small middle bedroom and my bed was the couch in the living room.

The man started yelling at me saying, "You aren't a fit mother for your sons! You're nothing but a whore! . . . ." and continued with the tirades until I was able to tell Kyle to get him out my house. Kyle was going to take him back to Salt Lake City and come back to get the rest of his friends and then visit with his children. This is when my mother showed up.

With the help of J.D., we loaded up clothes, kids and as much as my Mom's old Chevy Sedan could hold in her trunk and got out as soon as we could. We looked for a red and white pickup going the direction of Wendover, but never saw one, much to our relief. We quickly unloaded Darleen and all of her affects at Grandma Nelson's and Mom explained very bluntly why I was leaving Kyle. "He caused her to commit adultery," was her honest explanation, and my Grandma understood while I hung my head in shame.

We then thought it best that we leave immediately in case Kyle caught on to our plans and came over to get us.

We said our goodbyes, and hugs and kisses and started on our way home to California.

The beautiful blood-red sun was going down in the west against the stark Rocky Mountains of the Great Salt Lake Valley as we headed toward California in my Mom's blue'79 Chevy Sedan. I nursed John while falling asleep. The kids made themselves as comfortable as they could be in the back seat. It would be a long trip home.

I now had God's promise when he said to me, "All that I have is yours, Carla."